BRIDGET MARRISON

TENNIS

A NEW FAN'S GUIDE TO THE GAME, THE TOURNAMENTS AND THE PLAYERS

Note

Whilst every effort has been made to ensure that the content of this book is as technically accurate and as sound as possible, neither the author nor the publishers can accept responsibility for any injury or loss sustained as a result of the use of this material.

Published by A&C Black Publishers Ltd
36 Soho Square, London W1D 3QY
www.acblack.com

ISBN 978 1 4081 1901 3

A CIP catalogue record for this book is available from the British Library.

Acknowledgements
Cover photographs © PAPhotos
Cover design by James Watson
All photographs @ Mike Frey excepting:
Getty Images pp. **19l**, **44c**, **46bl**; Ray Giubilo pp. **12t**, **13**, **14br**, **18b**, **19cr**, **28**, **29tr/br**, **31br**, **33**, **39**, **41br**, **42c/r**, **43br**, **45**, **47br**, **49**, **50t**, **51c**, **59r**, **70**, **71tr**, **74–5**, **76–7**, **78–9**, **80**, **82**, **84–5**, **86–7**, **88**, **89tr**, **90tl/tc/tr/bl/bc**, **91tl/tc/bl/bc/br**, **101tl**, **110bl**, **115tr/br**; Tommy Hindley@Professional Sport pp. **17l/r**, **18t**, **21r**, **40t**, **51b**, **81**, **83**, **90br**, **93c/b**, **95t.** (t = top; b = bottom; c= centre; l = left; r = right)

Inside design by Stephanie Peat and Andrew Mountain

This book is produced using paper that is made from wood grown in managed, sustainable forests. It is natural, renewable and recyclable. The logging and manufacturing processes conform to the environmental regulations of the country of origin.

Printed and bound in China by C&C Joint Printing Co., (SHANG HAI) Ltd.

WELCOME

was 16 years old when I first visited The Championships at Wimbledon and got the tennis bug. I guess it wasn't surprising when you live near one of the best tennis venues in the world. Since then I have been fortunate enough as a publisher to follow the Tour around the world and feed that bug.

Tennis is one of the most exciting and vibrant sports. At the moment it is bursting with great players and historic rivalries. While Wimbledon remains the jewel in the crown of British Tennis, the arrival of the ATP World Tour Finals in London in 2009 gave British fans the opportunity to watch some of the best players in the world on the hard courts of the O2 Arena in London's Docklands.

The global game has never been more fascinating. The men and women's Tours now take in destinations from Auckland in New Zealand to Belgrade in Serbia and the players represent over 100 countries. The current rivalries in the men's game are up

there with some of the best ever. Roger Federer is arguably the greatest player of all time. The women's game has its own stars who will be an inspiration for all young women who want to compete in sport and life.

One of the challenges of writing this book was the decision about what to include from a sport that is steeped in history and constantly changing, not to mention the players who have skill levels that take your breath away. I have focused on tennis post 1968 when amateurs and professionals started competing together, for this is when the sport really took off. Since then prize money has flowed, broadcast and sponsorship rights are invaluable assets and the sport's governing bodies have professionalised the Tour.

A book like this could not have come about without the assistance of an amazing team. Stephanie Peat is one of the best art editors I have had the pleasure to work with; Michael Beattie helped create and shape some of the

chapters and Rob McLean subbed the pages with unbounded enthusiasm and knowledge. The images are stunning and my thanks extend to Mike Frey not only for his inspiration and encouragement, but also for supplying most of the pictures as seen through his lense; Tommy Hindley and Ray Giubilo for their great photos of the less recent players and events. Finally, many thanks to Lucy Beevor and Charlotte Atyeo at A&C Black for making it happen.

The book is packed full of statistics and I have endeavoured to ensure they are correct. However as with any such project, if you find the odd error, I would be grateful if you would contact me at tennishead where I am publisher, (bmarrison@tennishead.net) with details or with any suggestions of how we might improve future editions.

Happy Reading!

BRIDGET MARRISON

6

54

56

96

30

CONTENTS

THE BASICS

Tennis is a sport played between two players (singles) or between two pairs (doubles) on a rectangular court. The players use rackets to strike a hollow rubber ball covered with felt, usually yellow, over a net into the opponent's court.

Tennis is played and enjoyed by many people around the world — from the age of three to 93

ennis has a rich and colourful history. Although its roots are the subject of several theories, it was probably first played by monks in their monastery cloisters.

Today the sport is a multi-million pound global game that attracts professional players who travel round the world with the Tour. To make it to the top of such a competitive sport, players focus on tennis from an early age.

Millions of people around the world play the game for fun — from the age of three to 93. There are special courts and balls for juniors, there is strong participation from wheelchair players and there are variations of the game for the visually impaired and the deaf. Tennis is an inclusive sport. For the recreational player tennis is also a great way of socialising. Tennis clubs are often focal points for communities organising off court events for members. ➜

ESSENCE OF THE GAME

Andy Murray, British No1 who has risen as high as No.2 in the world

The Chair Umpire oversees the match

Britain's Jamie Murray with Serbia's Jelena Jankovic, 2007 Wimbledon Mixed Doubles champions

DID YOU KNOW?
It is usual to shake hands with your opponent at the end of a match.

Players show their respect at the end of a match

↓ THE FUNDAMENTALS

1 TECHNIQUE

Tennis is a technical game. A great player needs good technique to execute the strokes.

2 SEVEN KEY STROKES

To have an all-round game players need to master the serve, return, forehand, backhand, volley, lob and drop shot.

3 FITNESS

Players undergo demanding fitness training to enable them to endure long matches in tough climates.

4 MENTAL STRENGTH

Great players develop strong minds to outplay their opponents even when they are under extreme pressure.

❝ I have always considered tennis as a combat in an arena between two players who have their rackets and courage as weapons ❞

YANNICK NOAH, FRENCH TENNIS PLAYER

Ana Ivanovic, winner at Roland Garros in 2008

Roger Federer kisses the trophy at Roland Garros

Doubles players on a grass court

> ❝ What is the single most important quality in a tennis champion? I would have to say desire, staying in there and winning matches even when you are not playing that well ❞

JOHN MCENROE, AMERICAN TENNIS LEGEND AND COMMENTATOR

It is a game that is easy to follow but you have to get to grips with some of the jargon. Take the scoring of 15, 30, 40. In other racket sports such as badminton and squash this would simply be 1, 2, 3. Some of the phrases date back to its roots, but tennis is simple to understand.

The professional tennis tours are today organised by governing bodies at national and international level and even today the game is changing, with the professional calendar being re-drawn to allow players a longer off season. The four major events, known as the Grand Slams, give tennis its highest profile.

The biggest change to the modern game came in 1968 when amateurs and professionals started playing the same events. This was the start of the Open era and the game has thrived ever since.

More money and sponsorship has come into the game and places have been added to the Tour, introducing players from emerging nations and economies such as India and China, Serbia and Croatia.

Tennis is a game with a marvellous history and it has a bright future. Millions of people around the world have fallen in love with the game of tennis. Now is your chance. ●

KIT YOU NEED

1. SHOES

2. RACKET

3. CLOTHES

4. BALLS

Rafael Nadal celebrates victory on the red clay

Tennis for everyone, junior players celebrate

DOUBLES LINES

SINGLES LINES

← SERVICE LINE

← BASELINE

↑ CENTRE SERVICE LINE

THE COURT

Although courts can have different surfaces, they have standard dimensions

Although tennis courts can have different surfaces they are a standard size. The court is 78 feet (23.7 metres) long and for singles 27 feet (8.23 metres) wide, for doubles the court is 36 feet (10.97 metres) wide.

The net at the centre of the court is 3 feet (0.9 metres) high.

As well as the dimensions of the court the International Tennis Federation stipulates that there must be a minimum amount of room around a championship court. This is 21 feet (6.4 metres) between the baseline and the back fence at each end and 12 feet (3.7 metres) each side.

A court built at a tennis club or park for recreational use may have less space around it, but apart from that, the actual playing areas won't be any different to the court that the professionals play on. ●

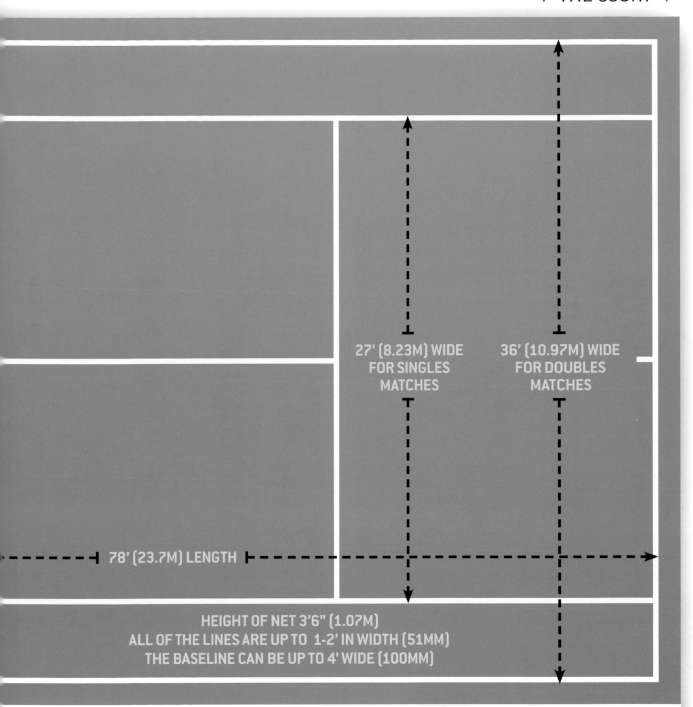

27' (8.23M) WIDE
FOR SINGLES
MATCHES

36' (10.97M) WIDE
FOR DOUBLES
MATCHES

78' (23.7M) LENGTH

HEIGHT OF NET 3'6" (1.07M)
ALL OF THE LINES ARE UP TO 1-2' IN WIDTH (51MM)
THE BASELINE CAN BE UP TO 4' WIDE (100MM)

Sharapova won
Wimbledon in 2004
at the age of 17

66 A great tennis career is something
that a 15 year old normally doesn't
have. I hope my example helps other
teens believe they can accomplish
things they never thought possible 99

MARIA SHARAPOVA, RUSSIAN PLAYER AND
TEENAGE GRAND SLAM WINNER

JAMES BLAKE

6' 9" tall, American Sam Querrey possesses a huge serve

COMPETITIVE

There is a clear structure to the professional tour and a fair amount of jargon in tennis, but once you grasp the basics it is easy

Beach Tennis is an internationally recognised form of tennis competition

P rofessional tennis players are organised by governing bodies. The International Tennis Federation (ITF) is responsible for running competitions from the top level — that's Olympic tennis and the four Grand Slams — to the entry level ITF Men's Satellite and Futures Circuit and the ITF Women's circuit. There are also ITF circuits and team events for juniors, seniors, beach tennis and wheelchair tennis players.

Men and women play on different tours organised by their respective governing body. The men's body is called the Association of Tennis Professionals (ATP) and the women's

Players, umpire and referee watch the coin toss at the start of a match

DID YOU KNOW?
In the 2004 Masters Cup Roger Federer defeated Marat Safin in a tiebreak that had 38 points. Federer won 20-18.

GAME

THE TOSS
At the start of a match a coin toss decides which player will serve first. The player that wins the toss can choose to serve or receive. At amateur level the coin toss is often replaced by a spin of the racket.

governing body is the Women's Tennis Association (WTA). The logos for both of these organisations often appear at tournaments.

The ATP and WTA are responsible for the Challenger Circuit. These tournaments are below the Tour. When a professional player is starting out they begin on the Challenger Circuit before progressing to the main Tour.

Both of the professional Tours have events at different levels. The men and women's events have different names but in essence they are simply categorised by prize money and the number of players that enter. The better a player, the higher the level of tournament they play. Professional players typically play between 18 and 30 events a year.

The men's Tour is split into events called ATP World Tour Finals, ATP Masters 1000 Events, ATP 500 Events, ATP 250 Events and Challengers.

The women's events are either Premier or International.

JARGON BUSTER

ACE
A valid serve that the receiver is unable to return. When the receiver is unable even to touch the ball this is known as a full ace.

ADVANTAGE
The point after an even score of 40-all (deuce). The winner of this point gains an advantage and need only win the next point to take the game.

BREAK
When one player has a lead of two games. Winning a game as a receiver has come to be known – incorrectly – as "making the break". If the player who has suffered the service break then wins the next game as receiver, this is known as "breaking back".

CHANGEOVER
Players change ends at the end of the first game of the set and then every other game i.e. after every uneven numbered game. A changeover after the end of the set only occurs if the number of games in the completed set is uneven. Otherwise the changeover takes place after the first game of the following set.

GAME
A game consists of four points 15, 30, 40 and game. If both players have scored three points each, the score is called "deuce" and the next point gives the "advantage" to the next player scoring it. If that player then wins the next point he also wins the game. If the other player wins the score returns to deuce and goes on until one players wins two points after deuce.

LOVE GAME
A game in which the loser has not won any points.

MATCH
The number of sets played in a match can vary. Most often women play the best of three sets, so a player wins with two sets. Men's matches can be the best of three sets or the best of five sets.

NOT UP
The term for a ball that has bounced twice before being returned by the player, who loses the point.

SERVE
A player gets two chances for each point to get the serve into the service box and into play.

FIRST SERVE
The first ball the server attempts to put into play.

ROGER FEDERER

DINARA SAFINA

GORAN IVANISEVIC

DID YOU KNOW?
In 1996 Goran Ivanisevic served 1477 Aces in the season.

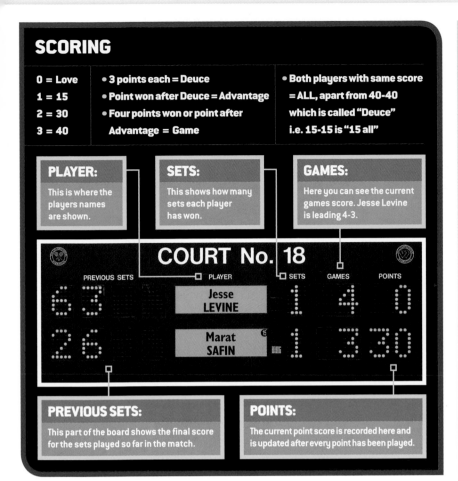

SCORING

0 = Love	• 3 points each = Deuce	• Both players with same score = ALL, apart from 40-40
1 = 15	• Point won after Deuce = Advantage	which is called "Deuce"
2 = 30	• Four points won or point after	i.e. 15-15 is "15 all"
3 = 40	Advantage = Game	

PLAYER:
This is where the players names are shown.

SETS:
This shows how many sets each player has won.

GAMES:
Here you can see the current games score. Jesse Levine is leading 4-3.

COURT No. 18

PREVIOUS SETS	PLAYER	SETS	GAMES	POINTS
6 3	Jesse LEVINE	1	4	0
2 6	Marat SAFIN	1	3	30

PREVIOUS SETS:
This part of the board shows the final score for the sets played so far in the match.

POINTS:
The current point score is recorded here and is updated after every point has been played.

JARGON BUSTER

SECOND SERVE
The second and final chance for a player to serve the ball into play.

FAULT
A serve that fails to land in the opposing service area.

DOUBLE FAULT
Two consecutive serves where the ball does not end up in opposing service area.

FOOT FAULT
A fault caused by the server's foot touching or crossing the service line or centre mark before the racket touches the ball.

NET OR LET SERVICE
When the server hits a ball that lands within the service box but that touches the net as it goes over, the serve is taken again. (If the ball touches the net and lands outside the service box the serve is not taken again, but is a fault).

RETURN
An abbreviation for "return of serve" where the player who receives serve plays the ball back to the opponent.

RALLY
The play that occurs between the players following the return of serve.

OUT
The call given when a ball does not land on or in the required boundary (balls that are "in" are not called).

SET
A set is made up of a minimum of six games. The winner is the first player to reach six games with a two game margin (if the set is tied at six games all a tie-break is played).

TIE-BREAK
A means of determining the winner of a set tied at six games all. The winner is the first player to reach seven points with a margin of at least two points over the other player. Ordinary numbers are used to score the points during a tie break. In doubles when the two teams are tied at one set each a super tie-break is played in ten points with a two-point margin.

Professional players enter these events and in addition to prize money they win ranking points, which are awarded on the basis of how far a player progresses in the tournament.

DID YOU KNOW?
In 2004 in the first round of the French Open Fabrice Santoro defeated Arnaud Clement in a match that lasted 6 hours and 33 minutes 6-4 6-3 6-7(5) 3-6 16-14.

ARNAUD CLEMENT

The player with the most points is deemed the world No.1. Getting to the top of the world rankings is one measure of a player's success. Equally, winning a tournament is also a reflection of a player's success, most notably where a player wins a Grand Slam event.

Both the ATP and the WTA are responsible for an annual calendar of events around the world. One of the realities of being a professional tennis player is that they must travel to all of the events. The calendar starts in January and ends in either November or December, so players do get some time for themselves at the end of the year. This is known as the "off season", when there is no competitive play.

The same thing happens at every level of play. For example, a player starting out at a national level will travel around the country to play events. In Great Britain the governing body is the LTA (Lawn Tennis Association). ●

DID YOU KNOW?
In a set where a player does not win a game, officially it is known as a love game, unofficially it is known as a "bagel". If a player loses two sets to love then unofficially it is a "double bagel"!

Suzanne Lenglen (right) with "Molla" Mallory at Wimbledon in 1922

DID YOU KNOW?
The word "deuce" probably comes from the French "a deux" (meaning two) because two more points are required to win.

Wooden rackets are history. Racket technology has changed the way we play

HISTORY

The game of tennis has come a long way from when it was first played by French monks

The sport as it exists today has its roots in the second half of the 19th century but it is possible to find some games that are similar to tennis much further back in time.

Monks in France probably played the first game of tennis. The game was called "jeu de paume" (game of the palm) because the small hard ball was hit over the net with the hand. Later, players of jeu de paume started to wear a glove to protect the hand and eventually a simple wooden racket was developed.

In the 1530s King Henry VIII built a tennis court at Hampton Court for "real tennis" which was played throughout Europe, mainly by kings and their courtiers.

Fast-forward to the 19th century when a game called "rackets" was introduced. Players used a long handled racket and a small hard white ball. Two keen players called Harry Gem and Augurio Perera invented an outdoor version of the game, which they called "lawn tennis". It is widely believed that the first lawn tennis club opened in Leamington Spa, England, in 1872 as a result of the increased popularity of the game.

The person most associated with developing the modern game of tennis is Major Walter Clopton Wingfield. In 1873 he developed a game that was simpler than "rackets" but was played outside. He manufactured a portable box, which contained everything needed to play the game. Although he called it "sphairistike", (from the Greek word for ball games) it became better known as "lawn tennis". In his boxes there were two net posts, a net, rackets and India rubber balls plus instructions about laying out the court and how to play.

Each of Wingfield's boxes cost five guineas, about £5.25, which in those days

Jack Kramer, who won the Wimbledon title in 1947

BILL TILDEN

DID YOU KNOW?

The score "love" may come from the French l'oeuf (egg) which symbolises "nothing". While the English mispronounced "l'oeuf"as "love" the French reverted back to "zero".

DID YOU KNOW?

In 1316 it is thought that French King Louis X died after a strenuous game of tennis.

was a lot of money. The game continued to be played mainly by the wealthy classes. The following year sphairistike was taken from the UK to the USA by two brothers, Clarence and Joseph Clark, and a tournament was played in America.

In 1877 the All England Club held its first tournament, where some of the croquet lawns had been converted into tennis courts. From then on tennis tournaments were staged around the world. Those tournaments were the forerunners of today's Grand Slam events.

Before 1968 the game was essentially played by amateurs and as each country held its own tournament, players travelled to them at their own expense. There are lots of famous players from this period, referred to as before the "Open Era".

The most notable amateur players were Donald Budge, Jack Crawford, Jack Kramer (above), Bill Tilden (right) and among the women Suzanne Lenglen, who is often viewed as the first real superstar of tennis. In 1919 she won the first of 12 titles at what were to become the Slams. With her elegant style she raised the profile of the sport, adding a touch of glamour.

For the modern game 1968 is the most significant date. The first official "Open" tournament took place in Bournemouth, UK. It was open to entries from both amateurs and professionals. The first Grand Slam was the French Open and Ken Rosewall won both events. Rod Laver was the first man to win each of the Grand Slam events in the same year. Since then there have also been many additions to the way the game is played, such as the introduction of tie-breaks to Grand Slam tennis in 1970.

Not only has the game itself evolved over time, but so have tennis rackets. Originally manufactured with wooden frames containing strings that were

made of dried twisted animal gut, in the 1970s oversized metal rackets became popular. Today most rackets are made from lightweight carbon fibre and have large heads to enable better contact with the ball.

The introduction of new racket technology has also changed the way the game is played and the potential for players to create spin on the ball and to serve the ball at breakneck speeds. The tennis players of the 1920s would be astonished at the speed and power of the ball in the modern game.

Today's players have also become athletes. To reach the top of the game they have to achieve peak physical fitness, a far cry from the early days of legendary eating and drinking by the players before matches.

Tennis is now one of the biggest professional sports for both men and women and the Tour attracts players from many countries. ●

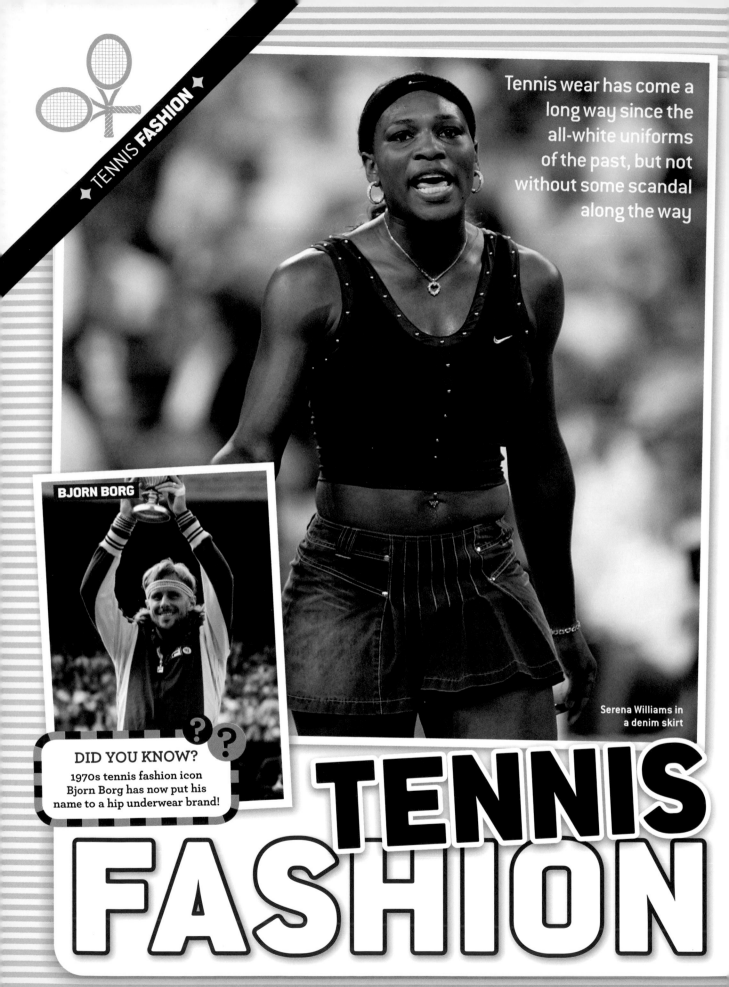

Tennis wear has come a long way since the all-white uniforms of the past, but not without some scandal along the way

BJORN BORG

DID YOU KNOW?

1970s tennis fashion icon Bjorn Borg has now put his name to a hip underwear brand!

Serena Williams in a denim skirt

TENNIS FASHION

Gussy Moran caused a stir in 1949

VENUS WILLIAMS

ANDRE AGASSI

MARIA SHARAPOVA

DID YOU KNOW?

During his playing days, Rene Lacoste was nicknamed "the crocodile" after winning a crocodile-skin suitcase in a bet. His clothing brand still sports a crocodile logo to this day.

Tennis and fashion have shared a love-hate relationship that dates back to the early 20th century. Times have certainly moved on from the uniform of all-white slacks and sweaters and below-the-knee skirts of the 1920s to the multicoloured T-shirted men and miniskirted women of today, but not without some scandalous moments along the way.

The idea that a man wearing shorts on a tennis court could cause controversy seems ludicrous now, but there was uproar when Bunny Austin did so at the US Open in 1932. It was not to be the last time that the powers that be failed to recognise the benefits of function over form when it came to tennis attire.

Austin's shorts were long forgotten – and widely adopted – by the time "Gorgeous" Gussy Moran caused outrage at Wimbledon sporting lace-lined knickers under her short skirt in 1949. Photographers laid down flat on the side of the court to shoot the offending underwear! After that, there was little left that could shock the tennis authorities, although plenty of players tested the limits of the rules over the coming years.

The advent of regular tennis television coverage from 1970 forced tennis authorities to do away with the ➜

> 66 **Gussy Moran caused outrage at Wimbledon sporting lace-lined knickers under her short skirt in 1949** 99

American
Bethanie Mattek-Sands
at Wimbledon

DID YOU KNOW?
In 2002 German player
Tommy Haas was sent off
court at Flushing Meadows for
wearing a sleeveless T-shirt.

Rafael Nadal in
sleeveless t-shirt
and Capri pants

Roger Federer in cardigan with "RF" crest at Wimbledon

66 Up until 2009, Nadal always sported long capri pants and sleeveless t-shirts – which were still banned up until 2002 99

traditional all-white dress code, as viewers couldn't tell which player was which on the small screens. When pastel colours were permitted at that year's US Open to help the audience, the technicolour floodgates opened – except at Wimbledon, who to this day insist that players wear predominantly white on court.

Soon tennis fashion became all the rage, both on and off court. Such was the impact of the clothes worn by the likes of John McEnroe, Vitas Gerulaitis and Bjorn Borg in the 1970s and 1980s that a whole new audience was introduced to the sport. Three decades later, Borg's famous pinstripe Wimbledon shirt and red tracksuit top are still regarded as cool retro casual wear.

Many sports brands have re-released outdated tennis shoes, such as the Adidas Forest Hills range, named after the New York region that staged the US Open until 1977. More fashionable than functional, the shoes are billed as casual street wear. Similarly, the Fred Perry and Lacoste collections are now better known for their street fashion appeal than their on-court focus, although both brands still kit out top professionals.

Today, tennis clothing is mainly functional with added flourishes, although a number of high-profile players and their sponsors devote a little more time to perfecting a signature look. Maria Sharapova has played in a number of eveningwear-inspired skirts, such as a dress encrusted with 600 Swarovski crystals and a tuxedo-themed outfit. Serena Williams has played wearing a denim skirt and a skintight black catsuit. Up until 2009, Rafael Nadal always sported long capri pants and sleeveless T-shirts – which were still banned up until 2002.

Perhaps the most high-profile tennis fashion moment each season is the unveiling of Roger Federer's Wimbledon outfit. Memorably, the Swiss arrived on court in long white trousers and a cardigan in 2008, bringing tennis fashion full circle. ●

MARIA SHARAPOVA

SUZANNE LENGLEN

SERENA WILLIAMS

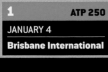

1	ATP 250
JANUARY 4	
Brisbane International	

2	ATP 250
JANUARY 12	
Medibank International, Sydney	

3	Grand Slam
JANUARY 19	
Australian Open, Melbourne	

4	ATP 250
FEBRUARY 16	
Open 13, Marseille	

5	ATP 500
FEBRUARY 23	
Barclays Dubai Tennis Championships, Dubai	

6	Davis Cup
MARCH 6	
Benidorm	

7	ATP 1000
MARCH 12	
Indian Wells, California	

8	ATP 1000
MARCH 25	
Sony Ericsson Open, Miami, Florida	

9	ATP 1000
APRIL 12	
Rolex Masters, Monte Carlo	

10	ATP 1000
APRIL 27	
Internazionali BNL d'Italia, Rome	

11	ATP 250
MAY 4	
Serbia Open, Belgrade	

ROGERS CUP

The tennis governing bodies publish a schedule of events at the beginning of the season. Each player selects the events he will play.

US OPEN

THE MEN'S TOUR

In 2009 Novak Djokovic travelled an estimated 62,000 miles to play in 17 Tour events, four Grand Slams and a Davis Cup tie

ROLAND GARROS

INDIAN WELLS

AUSTRALIAN OPEN

12	**ATP 1000**
MAY 11	
Mutua Madrilena Madrid Open, Madrid	

13	**Grand Slam**
MAY 24	
Roland Garros, Paris	

14	**ATP 250**
JUNE 8	
Gerry Weber Open, Halle	

15	**Grand Slam**
JUNE 22	
The Championsh... Wimbledon, Lond...	

16	**ATP 1000**
AUGUST 8	
Rogers Cup, Montreal	

17	**ATP 1000**
AUGUST 16	
Western & Southern Financial Group Masters, Cincinnati, Ohio	

18	**Grand Slam**
AUGUST 31	
US Open, Flushing Meadows, New York	

19	**ATP 1000**
OCTOBER 12	
Shanghai Masters, Shanghai	

20	**ATP 500**
NOVEMBER 2	
Davidoff Swiss Indoors, Basel	

21	**ATP 1000**
NOVEMBER 8	
BNP Paribas Masters, Paris	

22	**ATP Final**
NOVEMBER 22	
Barclays ATP World Tour Finals, London	

MILEOMETER

HOMETOWN: Belgrade, Serbia (see page 58)

1 Brisbane, Australia = 9,575 miles/15,408km
2 Sydney, Australia = 453 miles/730km
3 Melbourne, Australia = 443 miles/712km
4 Marseille, France = 10,437 miles/16,796km
5 Dubai, UAE = 3,283 miles/5,283km
6 Benidorm, Spain = 3,324 miles/5,349km
7 Indian Wells, USA = 5,981 miles/9,626km
8 Miami, USA = 2,221 miles/3,574km
9 Monte Carlo, Monaco = 4,892 miles/7,873km
10 Rome, Italy = 287 miles/462km
11 Belgrade, Serbia = 448 miles/722km

12 Madrid, Spain = 1,260 miles/2,027km
13 Paris, France = 655 miles/1,053km
14 Halle, Germany = 464 miles/747km
15 Wimbledon, UK = 525 miles/845km
16 Montreal, Canada = 3,241 miles/5,216km
17 Cincinnati, USA = 706 miles/1,136km
18 New York, NY = 563 miles/906km
19 Shanghai, China = 7,364 miles/11,851km
20 Basel, Switzerland = 5,622 miles/9,047km
21 Paris, France = 258 miles/416km
22 London, UK = 212 miles/341km

TOTAL
22 events,
62,214 miles,
100,123km

1	International
JANUARY 5	
ASB Classic, Auckland	

2	Premier
JANUARY 11	
Medibank International, Sydney	

3	Grand Slam
JANUARY 19	
Australian Open, Melbourne	

4	Fed Cup
FEBRUARY 1	
Tallinn	

5	International
FEBRUARY 9	
PTT Pattaya Women's Open, Pattaya City	

6	International
FEBRUARY 15	
Regions Morgan Keegan, Memphis, Tennesee	

7	Premier
MARCH 11	
Indian Wells, California	

8	Premier
MARCH 25	
Sony Ericsson Open, Miami, Florida	

9	International
APRIL 6	
MPS Group Championships, Ponte Vedra Beach, Florida	

10	Premier
APRIL 13	
Family Circle Cup, Charleston, South Carolina	

11	Premier
APRIL 27	
Porsche Tennis Grand Prix, Stuttgart	

12	Premier
MAY 4	
Internazionali BNL d'Italia-Rome	

13	Premier
MAY 9	
Mutua Madrilena, Madrid Open, Madrid	

INDIAN WELLS

EASTBOURNE

AUSTRALIAN OPEN

PROFILE

Full Name: Caroline Wozniacki

Date of Birth: 11 July 1990

Birthplace: Odense, Denmark

Height: 5' 10" (178cm)

Weight: 128lbs (58kg)

Plays: Right-handed, two-handed backhand

Turned Pro: 2005

Website: www.carolinewozniacki.dk

In 2009 Caroline Wozniacki played 26 tournaments and travelled an estimated 70,000 miles

THE WOMEN'S TOUR

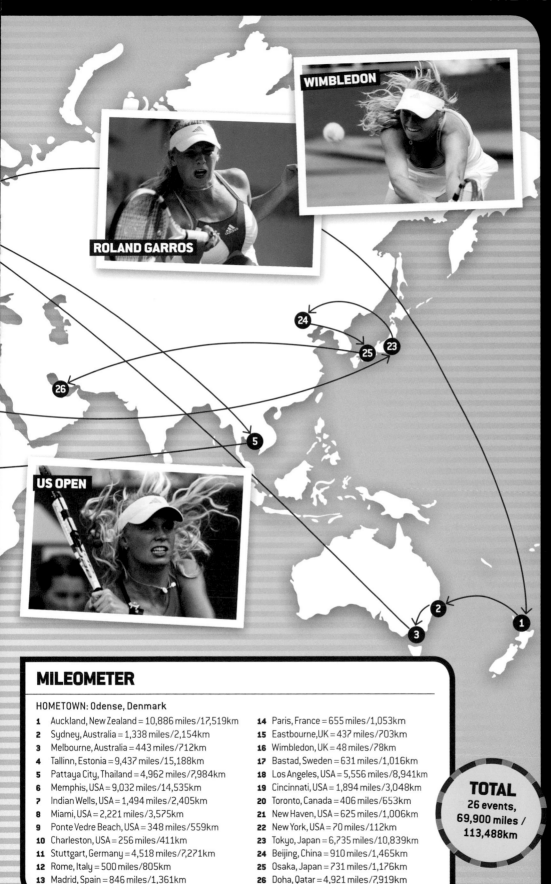

WIMBLEDON

ROLAND GARROS

US OPEN

14	Grand Slam
MAY 24	
Roland Garros, Paris	

15	Premier
JUNE 15	
AEGON International, Eastbourne	

16	Grand Slam
JUNE 22	
The Championships, Wimbledon, London	

17	International
JULY 6	
Swedish Open Women, Bastad	

18	Premier
AUGUST 3	
East West Bank Classic, Los Angeles, California	

19	Premier
AUGUST 10	
Western & Southern Financial Group, Women's Open, Cincinnati, Ohio	

20	Premier
AUGUST 17	
Rogers Cup, Toronto	

21	Premier
AUGUST 23	
Pilot Pen Tennis New Haven, Connecticut	

22	Grand Slam
AUGUST 31	
Flushing Meadows, New York	

23	Premier
SEPTEMBER 28	
Toray Pan Pacific Open, Tokyo	

24	Premier
OCTOBER 3	
China Open, Beijing	

25	International
OCTOBER 12	
Japan Women's Open, Osaka	

26	Premier
OCTOBER 26	
Sony Ericsson Championships, Doha	

MILEOMETER

HOMETOWN: Odense, Denmark

1 Auckland, New Zealand = 10,886 miles/17,519km
2 Sydney, Australia = 1,338 miles/2,154km
3 Melbourne, Australia = 443 miles/712km
4 Tallinn, Estonia = 9,437 miles/15,188km
5 Pattaya City, Thailand = 4,962 miles/7,984km
6 Memphis, USA = 9,032 miles/14,535km
7 Indian Wells, USA = 1,494 miles/2,405km
8 Miami, USA = 2,221 miles/3,575km
9 Ponte Vedre Beach, USA = 348 miles/559km
10 Charleston, USA = 256 miles/411km
11 Stuttgart, Germany = 4,518 miles/7,271km
12 Rome, Italy = 500 miles/805km
13 Madrid, Spain = 846 miles/1,361km
14 Paris, France = 655 miles/1,053km
15 Eastbourne, UK = 437 miles/703km
16 Wimbledon, UK = 48 miles/78km
17 Bastad, Sweden = 631 miles/1,016km
18 Los Angeles, USA = 5,556 miles/8,941km
19 Cincinnati, USA = 1,894 miles/3,048km
20 Toronto, Canada = 406 miles/653km
21 New Haven, USA = 625 miles/1,006km
22 New York, USA = 70 miles/112km
23 Tokyo, Japan = 6,735 miles/10,839km
24 Beijing, China = 910 miles/1,465km
25 Osaka, Japan = 731 miles/1,176km
26 Doha, Qatar = 4,921 miles/7,919km

TOTAL
26 events,
69,900 miles /
113,488km

Monte Carlo Country Club, Monaco

Possibly the most beautiful club in the world, it hosts an ATP Masters event in April. The MCCC is situated on the slopes of Mont Agel, 810 metres above sea level, and has a panoramic view over the Mediterranean Sea. The art deco clubhouse was built in 1928. There are 21 clay courts.

STADIA

The tour travels around the world, taking the players to some breathtaking stadia and tennis clubs

← Rexall Centre, Toronto, Ontario, Canada

The Rexall Centre is at York University and has 16 courts with 12,500 seats in the main stadium. It hosts the men's or women's Rogers Cup every year.

Rothenbaum Tennis Centre, Hamburg, Germany →

Situated in the heart of the German city, next to the Outer Alster Lake, the Rothenbaum Tennis Centre is one of the oldest tennis facilities. The main court can seat 13,200 spectators and has a beautiful retractable roof.

DID YOU KNOW?

The Plaza de Toros de Las Ventas in Madrid, Spain, is normally used to stage bull-fights but in 2008 it hosted the Davis Cup tie between Spain and the USA.

La Caja Magica, Madrid, Spain →

"The Magic Box" has three main courts with retractable roofs in the same arena. In May it hosts a combined men and women's event.

← Indian Wells Tennis Garden, California, USA

Situated at the base of the Santa Rosa Mountains in Southern California. In March, the 80-acre tennis and entertainment facility hosts a combined men and women's event. It is the home of a regular tennis club with 11 sunken championship courts and a main stadium that can seat 16,000 people.

← Dubai Tennis Stadium, UAE

The hard courts of Dubai host a separate men and women's event in February. The main court seats 5,000 spectators who enjoy floodlit matches under clear desert skies.

Qi Zhong Stadium, Shanghai, China →

Located in the south west of Shanghai the Qi Zhong Tennis Centre was completed in 2006 and is Asia's largest tennis facility. The Centre Court Stadium can be covered by a unique eight-piece Magnolia Roof, which resembles a flower blooming when it opens. It has 15,000 seats. It hosts an ATP Masters Event in October.

← Crandon Park Tennis Centre, Miami, USA

Built in 1994 and moments away from Crandon Park Beach and adjacent to the Crandon Park Golf Club, the tennis centre has 26 courts. The main stadium can seat 14,000 spectators. It is home to the Sony Ericsson Open, a joint men's and women's event that takes place in March. It is often referred to as the "fifth slam" or the "Glam Slam" for its glamorous Miami location.

GRAND SLAM VENUES

Melbourne Park, Australia
The main stadium is the Rod Laver Arena.

Roland Garros, Paris, France
The main stadium is Philippe Chatrier.

All England Club, Wimbledon, UK
Centre Court seats 14,000 people.

Flushing Meadows, New York, USA
Arthur Ashe Stadium is the biggest tennis stadium in the world, holding 24,000 people.

GRAND SLAM

The term Grand Slam dates back to 1933, when Australian Jack Crawford managed to win the Australian Internationals, Roland Garros and Wimbledon. With the US Internationals fast approaching, *New York Times* journalist John Kieran wrote that if Crawford won this fourth title, "he would achieve on court the equivalent of a countered and vulnerable grand slam in bridge". Crawford lost in the final to Britain's Fred Perry, but the name was to go down in history.

Steffi Graf won 22 Grand Slam titles and is the only player to have completed a "Golden Slam"

THE GRAND

The four major tournaments in the tennis calendar are commonly known as the Grand Slams

The Grand Slam tournaments, also known as the Majors, are the most important tennis tournaments of the year in terms of ranking points, prestige and prize money. They are also the highest profile tournaments for the general public. There are four Grand Slam tournaments: the Australian Open, Roland Garros, the Championships at Wimbledon and the US Open.

Strictly speaking, while the phrase "Grand Slam" is often applied to describe each of the tournaments, the phrase actually refers to a player (or doubles team) who has won all four of the Majors – they are then said to have won the Grand Slam. Even more correct is that to be referred to as a Grand Slam winner, a player is required to have won each of the four majors in the same calendar year. It is an amazing feat for a player to win all four in the same calendar year, or even in the course of a career.

Each major singles competition starts with 128 competitors and over the course of a fortnight a player has to win seven consecutive matches. This is very demanding both mentally and physically, and the last rounds are normally contested among the world's best players.

TOURNAMENT DATES

- **Australian Open** January
- **Roland Garros** May/June
- **The Championships, Wimbledon** June/July
- **US Open** August/September

Under the seeding system – 32 players whose position in a tournament is arranged based on their ability/world ranking – the top players are kept apart until the later rounds, so in theory the number one seed would meet the second seed in the final, having played the number three or four seed in the semi-final and so on.

Each of the four Majors is played on a different surface, which makes further technical and tactical demands on a player's game.

Roger Federer has won more Grand Slam titles than any man in history

ALL-TIME MAJOR CHAMPIONS

MEN		WOMEN	
15	Roger Federer	24	Margaret Smith Court
14	Pete Sampras	22	Steffi Graf
12	Roy Emerson	19	Helen Wills Moody
11	Bjorn Borg	18	Martina Navratilova
11	Rod Laver	18	Chris Evert
10	Bill Tilden	12	Billie Jean King

Martina Navratilova, winner of 18 major titles

Pete Sampras, the 14-times champion

SLAMS

The Plexicushion at the Australian Open is a medium to medium-fast paced surface. The clay of Roland Garros is slower and potentially suits the baseline player. The grass of Wimbledon is fast and low-bouncing, traditionally suited to a player who serves and volleys. The hard Deco-Turf of the US Open is most similar to the hard surface of Australia but plays faster.

Each of the Grand Slam tournaments is the climax to the part of the season that has been played on that surface (often called a "swing"). There is a clay-court season leading up to the French Open, a grass-court season leading up to Wimbledon and so on, giving players the chance to play on the surface at lower level events before the Grand Slam.

The shortest gap between Major tournaments is between the French Open

WINNERS OF THE GRAND SLAM

1938	Don Budge
1953	Margaret Connolly
1962, 1969	Rod Laver
1970	Margaret Smith Court
1988	Steffi Graf

> " They are the most important tennis tournaments in the year in terms of ranking points, tradition and prize money "

and Wimbledon, which are played on two very different surfaces. As a result, it is a major achievement for a player to win back-to-back French Open and Wimbledon titles. Few players have done this.

In all Grand Slam events there are competitions for men's and ladies' singles, men's and ladies' doubles and mixed doubles. There is also a junior tournament, a legends event and a wheelchair event.

If a player not only wins all four Majors but also an Olympic gold medal, it is known as a Golden Slam. Steffi Graf is the only player in the Open Era to have achieved this when in 1988 she won all four Majors and an Olympic gold medal in Seoul, South Korea.

Andre Agassi has completed a career Golden Slam. He won each of the four majors and an Olympic gold medal, although not all in the same calendar year. ●

DID YOU KNOW?
The latest (or earliest!) ever finish to a match at the Aussie Open was 4.33am.

The famous blue plexi-cushion surface of the Hisense Arena under cover of the roof

STATISTICS
603,160 spectators
4,500 staff
337 ball kids
365 umpires
16,801 official towels sold
3,400 rackets strung
40km (25 miles) of string used
14 minutes – the fastest restring

AUSTRALIAN OPEN

The first Grand Slam of the year takes place in January at Melbourne Park and ensures the players get into gear early in the New Year

he Australian Open is the first major tournament of the calendar year and takes place mid-January during the Australian summer.

The first Australian Championships date back to 1905 and the event has a colourful history. Prior to the arrival at its current home Melbourne Park in 1988 the tournament was staged in different locations and at different times of year. At Melbourne Park it became the official first Grand Slam of the year and its dates in the calendar were fixed. It also moved from grass to a hard surface.

There is still some debate about whether the Australian Open falls too early in the year. Not only is the January weather in Melbourne unpredictable, it also comes very soon after the players have returned from the off-season. It means they have to get accustomed to competitive play soon after a prolonged period of practice or rest.

In response to the increased popularity of the game, Melbourne Park is undergoing a modernisation programme. This includes the installation of better seats, improved player facilities and a partly covered "town square" area with television screens for spectators outside the show courts. It will also see the addition of a roof to the Margaret Court Arena. The two main show courts already have retractable roofs that can move into place when needed.

The roofs over the courts protect against both wet weather and heat. In 2009 there were several days when the mercury hit over 40°C and matches were played under cover as part of the tournament's extreme heat policy.

> 66 **Prior to its arrival at Melbourne Park in 1988 the tournament was staged in different locations and at different times of year** 99

In 2009 Rafael Nadal won his first Australian Open title

MOST AUSTRALIAN TITLES IN OPEN ERA

MEN

4	Andre Agassi	1995, 2000, 2001, 2003
3	Roger Federer	2004, 2006, 2007
3	Mats Wilander	1983, 1984, 1988
2	Pete Sampras	1994, 1997
2	Ken Rosewall	1971, 1972
2	John Newcombe	1973, 1975
2	Jim Courier	1992, 1993
2	Boris Becker	1991, 1996
2	Ivan Lendl	1989, 1990
2	Stefan Edberg	1985, 1987
2	Guillermo Vilas	1978, 1979
2	Johan Kriek	1981, 1982

WOMEN

4	Serena Williams	2003, 2005, 2007, 2009
4	Steffi Graf	1988, 1989, 1990, 1994
4	Margaret Court*	1969, 1970, 1971, 1973
4	Monica Seles	1991, 1992, 1993, 1996
3	Martina Hingis	1997, 1998, 1999
2	Jennifer Capriati	2001, 2002
2	Martina Navratilova	1981, 1985
2	Chris Evert	1982, 1984
2	Hana Mandlikova	1982, 1987
2	Evonne Goolagong	1974, 1975

* won 7 titles pre 1969 as Margaret Smith

DID YOU KNOW?

In 1997 Martina Hingis became the ladies singles champion aged 16 years and three months.

AUSTRALIAN OPEN CHAMPIONS

YEAR	MEN	WOMEN
2009	Rafael Nadal	Serena Williams
2008	Novak Djokovic	Maria Sharapova
2007	Roger Federer	Serena Williams
2006	Roger Federer	Amelie Mauresmo
2005	Marat Safin	Serena Williams
2004	Roger Federer	Justine Henin
2003	Andre Agassi	Serena Williams
2002	Thomas Johansson	Jennifer Capriati
2001	Andre Agassi	Jennifer Capriati
2000	Andre Agassi	Lindsay Davenport

Maria Sharapova 2008 champion

The main show court was renamed the Rod Laver Arena in 2000. The Australian Rod Laver is one of the great names in tennis. He is the only man in the open era to have won a calendar year Grand Slam.

The most recent significant development was the introduction in 2008 of a very distinctive new blue playing surface. This is the "true blue" Plexicushion and is an acrylic surface, which gives a consistent bounce and is soft underfoot. The ball moves at a medium to medium-fast pace.

The playing sessions at the Aussie Open are split into day and night sessions, similar to the US Open. Spectators buy tickets for each session. The night sessions occasionally continue into the morning.

In 2008 Lleyton Hewitt played Marcos Baghdatis in a match that started at 11.47pm. At 4.33am, in the latest finish ever recorded at the Australian Open, Hewitt won 4-6 7-5 7-5 6-7 (4) 6-3. When the match finished there were still 15,000 spectators in the stadium. Tennis Australia, who have responsibility for organising the event, now have a policy not to start a match after 11pm.

Melbourne Park is scheduled to be home of the Australian Open until 2016. ●

STADIUM CAPACITIES

Rod Laver Arena	15,000
Hisense Arena	10,000
Margaret Court Arena	6,000
Show Court 2	3,000
Show Court 3	3,000

Court Philippe Chatrier: the main show court

Roger Federer finally conquered the clay in 2009

FRENCH WINNERS

2000 Mary Pierce
1983 Yannick Noah →
1967 Francoise Durr

ROLAND

Also known as the French Open, the clay-court major has produced great champions

The French Singles Men's Championships were first held in Paris in 1891 on the courts of the Stade Français Club. The women's singles were added six years later and in 1925 the tournament was open to entries from overseas players. The French Internationals were born and staged at the Stade Français and the Racing Club de France until the current tournament site at Roland Garros was opened in 1928.

The stadium at Roland Garros was built in response to the need for the French to have a venue where they could host the Davis Cup in 1928 after French tennis history had been made by Jacques "Toto" Brugnon, Jean Borota, Henri Cochet and Rene Lacoste.

The French Musketeers, as they became known, had beaten the Americans the previous year in the Davis Cup and needed somewhere to host the re-match. The Stade Français handed over three hectares of land near Porte d-Auteuil to the French Tennis Federation.

The handover of the land was accompanied by a request to name the new stadium after one of the Stade Français members who had died 10 years earlier. His name was Roland Garros.

The French tournament grew in stature until in 1968 it became the first Slam to embrace the "Open" era and open to amateurs and professionals. Unlike the other three Slams that were originally played on grass, the French Championships were always on clay.

It can be fun to watch play on clay, as it is a much slower surface than the other Slams. It can take the speed out of

Chris Evert won a record seven times at Roland Garros

MOST SINGLES TITLES IN OPEN ERA

MEN

6	Bjorn Borg	1974, 1975, 1978-1981
4	Rafael Nadal	2005-2008
3	Ivan Lendl	1984, 1986, 1987
3	Mats Wilander	1982, 1985, 1988
3	Gustavo Kuerten	1997, 2000, 2001

WOMEN

7	Chris Evert	1974, 1975, 1979, 1980, 1983, 1985, 1986
6	Steffi Graf	1987, 1988, 1993, 1995, 1996, 1999
4	Justine Henin	2003, 2005, 2006, 2007
3	Margaret Court	1969, 1970, 1973
3	Arantxa Sanchez Vicario	1989, 1994, 1998
3	Monica Seles	1990, 1991, 1992

ROLAND GARROS CHAMPIONS

GUSTAVO KUERTEN

Gustavo Kuerten's nickname was "Guga".
He won his first Slam on only his third attempt – a record in the Open era
He retired in May 2008
He speaks Portuguese, Spanish, English and French
After retiring he went to drama school

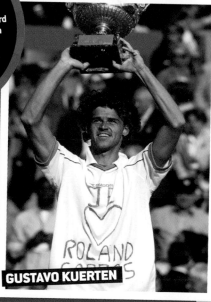

GUSTAVO KUERTEN

GARROS

> ❝ The French tournament grew in stature until in 1968 it became the first major to embrace the "Open" era ❞

the serve, giving the receiver more of a chance to win. This is why the great Pete Sampras never won at Roland Garros because his big serve became much less effective and it is why a steady baseline player like Chris Evert won the tournament a record seven times.

The main show court is Philippe Chatrier (named after one of the French Tennis Federation's presidents) which can hold 15,000 spectators. Court Suzanne Lenglen, built in 1995, seats 10,000 and the more intimate No.1 court has room for 4,500 spectators.

The park continues to undergo modernisation and in 2009 the French Tennis Federation announced plans to build a retractable roof for court Philippe Chartrier for the 2011 event. There's also a fabulous museum on site, tucked behind No.1 court, that is open most of the year. ●

YEAR	MEN	WOMEN
2009	Roger Federer	Svetlana Kuznetsova
2008	Rafael Nadal	Ana Ivanovic
2007	Rafael Nadal	Justine Henin
2006	Rafael Nadal	Justine Henin
2005	Rafael Nadal	Justine Henin
2004	Gaston Gaudio	Anastasia Myskina
2003	Juan Carlos Ferrero	Justine Henin
2002	Albert Costa	Serena Williams
2001	Gustavo Kuerten	Jennifer Capriati
2000	Gustavo Kuerten	Mary Pierce

STATISTICS
13,500 Men's
championship towels sold
200,000 glasses of Pimms consumed
26,500 kilos of strawberries eaten
20,000 Bottles of champagne opened
18,243 mini yellow tennis ball
keyrings sold
Over 54,200 Slazenger
balls used

WIMBLEDON

The Championships, Wimbledon are the only Grand Slam staged on grass and have been played since 1877

Andy Murray in determined mood at Wimbledon

The All England Club, which is responsible for staging the Championships, is a private club that was founded in 1868 originally as the "All England Croquet Club".

In 1875 lawn tennis, a game introduced by Major Walter Clopton Wingfield a year or so earlier and originally called Sphairistike, was added to the activities of the club. In the spring of 1877 the club was re-titled The All England Croquet and Lawn Tennis Club and signalled its change of name by instituting the first Lawn Tennis Championship. The only event held in 1877 was the gentleman's singles, won by Spencer Gore. About 200 spectators paid one shilling each to watch the final.

Each year local schools supply Ball boys and girls

The gates of the All England Lawn Tennis Club

WIMBLEDON FAST FACTS

The location's full name is the All England Lawn Tennis and Croquet Club.

The Club grounds consist of 19 grass courts.

The main court is the oval shaped Centre Court which can hold 15,000 spectators. The other key court for spectators is Court 1 with a capacity of just under 12,000.

A new Court 2 was built in 2009 to hold 4,000 people.

A new Court 3 was opened in 2010.

The All England Club will host the 2012 Olympic tennis event when the Games are held in London.

In Aorangi Park within the grounds there are 22 grass courts used for practice before and during the Championships and two acrylic courts.

Apart from the Centre Court and No.1 courts the courts are used year round by club members.

There are only 375 permanent members of the All England Club plus each year 100 players are appointed as temporary members.

Although the word croquet was dropped out of the title in 1882, it was restored in 1889 and the club has been known ever since as "The All England Lawn Tennis and Croquet Club".

In 1884 the Ladies Singles was established and Maud Watson beat a field of 13 players. The same year the gentlemen's doubles was launched.

Originally based on a site in Worple Road, Wimbledon, it was in 1922 that the 13-and-a-quarter acre ground at Wimbledon Park Road was opened. This is still the site of the Championships.

The Championships are now the only Grand Slam event held on grass. They occur each year during the last week of June and the first week of July and since 1982 have run over 13 days, with the middle Sunday normally being a rest day for the players, unless the weather has meant the tournament is behind schedule then it can become a day for competitive play.

The Championships have a colourful history but it was in August 1968, when both professionals and amateur players were allowed to enter the tournament that it became the modern championship ➔

> 66 **It was in 1922 that the 13 ¼ acre ground at Wimbledon Park Road was opened. This is still the site of the Championships today** 99

WIMBLEDON CHAMPIONS

YEAR	MEN	WOMEN
2009	Roger Federer	Serena Williams
2008	Rafael Nadal	Venus Williams
2007	Roger Federer	Venus Williams
2006	Roger Federer	Amelie Mauresmo
2005	Roger Federer	Venus Williams
2004	Roger Federer	Maria Sharapova
2003	Roger Federer	Serena Williams
2002	Lleyton Hewitt	Serena Williams
2001	Goran Ivanisevic	Venus Williams
2000	Pete Sampras	Venus Williams

Roger Federer has dominated
the event in recent years

THE QUEUE

The sight of people queuing for tickets is one of the iconic images of The Championships. That's because approximately 500 tickets each for Centre Court, No.1 and 2 courts are made available daily, except for the last four days. In addition 6,000 ground admission tickets are available each day and give access to the grounds and to unreserved seating and standing room on courts 3–19.

JUNIOR CHAMPIONSHIPS

The Junior Wimbledon Championships have been staged on grass during the second week of the Championships from 1947 to date, originally as an invitational event, but it was upgraded to Championship status in 1975.

Previous winners of the boy's title include Roger Federer (1998), Gael Monfils (2004) and Jeremy Chardy (2005). Junior Girls champions include Martina Hingis (1994), Amelie Mauresmo (1996) and Caroline Wozniacki (2006). British girl Laura Robson won the title in 2008.

British girl
Laura Robson

that it is today. In that year Rod Laver and Billie Jean King became the first Wimbledon Open champions. The total prize money for the tournament was £26,150.

The Lawn Tennis championship meeting – the Championships – comes under the joint management of the All England Tennis and Croquet Club (AELTC) and the Lawn Tennis Association (LTA).

In the last 20 years the grass at Wimbledon has played host to some of the most exciting players and rivalries the sport has ever seen. In 1980 Bjorn Borg became the first player to win the men's singles five successive times since the 1880s. Pete Sampras has won seven titles in total and in 2009 Roger Federer notched up his sixth title.

In 1985 Boris Becker became the youngest and first unseeded champion. The first wildcard (special admission to a tournament when lacking the standard qualifications) was Goran Ivanisevic in 2001, having lost three previous finals.

Other record holders include Martina Navratilova who in 1987 became the first player to win the ladies' singles six times in succession and in 1990 won her ninth ladies' singles title – a record that stands to this day. ●

> 66 **In the last 20 years Wimbledon has played host to the most exciting players and rivalries the sport has ever seen** 99

Serena Williams lifts the
Venus Rosewater Dish in 2009

DID YOU KNOW?
Britain's Virginia Wade
was the Wimbledon Ladies
Singles Champion in 1977.

The US Open moved to Flushing Meadows in 1978 and players have to contend with a famously noisy New York crowd

DID YOU KNOW?
1979 — Tracy Austin is the youngest women's champion aged 16 years 8 months 28 days.

US OPEN

The US Open presents the players with a unique set of challenges

The US Open is the last Grand Slam of the calendar year. It takes place in the final week of August and the first week of September. Since 1978 it has been staged at Flushing Meadows in New York on a hard surface called Deco Turf. This was not always the case as the US Open has the distinction among the Slams of being played on three different surfaces — grass, clay and hard.

The American Jimmy Connors is the only player to have won the US Open on all three surfaces. In 1974 he won the last time the Slam was played on grass and in 1976 Connors won on clay, a surface that only featured for three years. In 1978 he won on the hard courts of Flushing Meadows. That was the year the US Open moved from the West Side Club at Forest Hills.

The weather in New York at this time of year can be stifling and with the introduction of both day and night sessions the players have to be ready to play in the heat of the afternoon or the cooler, balmy night session. They also have to contend with the famously noisy New York crowd.

When night sessions were first introduced in 1975 the crowd witnessed one of the greatest comebacks in tennis history. The Spanish player Manuel Orantes saved five match points and came back from being down two sets to

Andre Agassi, who is married to the former women's champion Steffi Graf, celebrates winning his second US Open title in 1999

MOST SINGLES TITLES IN OPEN ERA

MEN

5	Jimmy Connors	1974, 1976, 1978, 1982, 1983
5	Pete Sampras	1990, 1993, 1995, 1996, 2002
5	Roger Federer	2004-2008
4	John McEnroe	1979-1981, 1984
3	Ivan Lendl	1985-1987

WOMEN

6	Chris Evert	1975-1978, 1980, 1982
5	Steffi Graf	1988, 1989, 1993, 1995, 1996
4	Billie Jean King	1967, 1971, 1972, 1974
4	Martina Navratilova	1983, 1984, 1986, 1987

US OPEN CHAMPIONS

YEAR	MEN	WOMEN
2009	Juan Martin del Potro	Kim Clijsters
2008	Roger Federer	Serena Williams
2007	Roger Federer	Justine Henin
2006	Roger Federer	Maria Sharapova
2005	Roger Federer	Kim Clijsters
2004	Roger Federer	Svetlana Kuznetsova
2003	Andy Roddick	Justine Henin
2002	Pete Sampras	Serena Williams
2001	Lleyton Hewitt	Venus Williams
2000	Marat Safin	Venus Williams

one and 0-5 in the fourth, to defeat Guillermo Vilas 4-6 1-6 6-2 7-5 6-4 in the semi-finals.

The US Open has a reputation for innovations that lead the tennis world. It was the first tournament to introduce equal prize money for men and women when in 1973 the Unites States Tennis Association took this bold step. In 2006 instant replay points were introduced. The spectators in the two main stadiums could see points replayed live on big screens.

The US Open is the culmination of a 10-week North American hard court season that is unique in terms of financial rewards. The US Open series, as the 10 tournaments that precede the Slam are known, offers additional prize money to the successful players. In 2005 Kim Clijsters won US$2.2 million for winning the US Open Series and US Open. This is the largest payout in women's sports history.

The last Slam of the year is unique among the Slams in that a tie-break determines the outcome of the match if the score reaches 6-6 in the final set. This became the norm in New York in 1970.

Attracting over 650,000 fans each year, the US Open is one of the most important sporting events in the US. It will remain one of the most challenging Slams for the players. ●

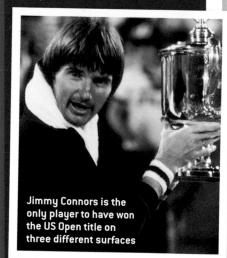

Jimmy Connors is the only player to have won the US Open title on three different surfaces

> ❝ You have the crowd here. You have the heat here. You have the noise here ❞
>
> BORIS BECKER, 1989 US OPEN CHAMPION

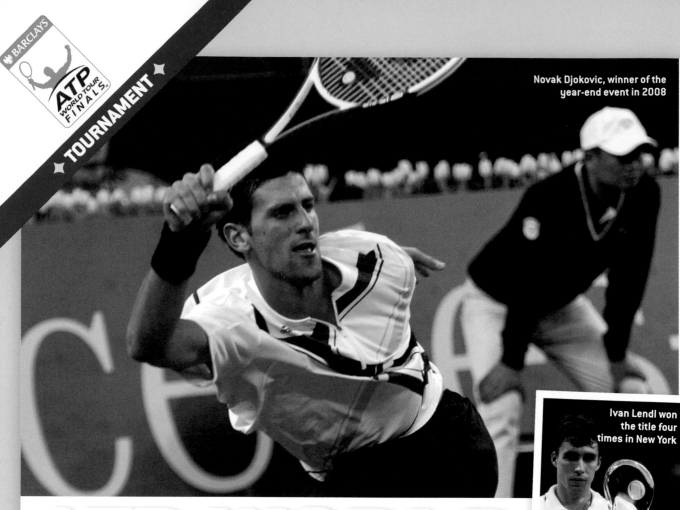

Novak Djokovic, winner of the year-end event in 2008

Ivan Lendl won the title four times in New York

ATP WORLD TOUR FINALS

The top eight men's singles and doubles players battle it out for season-end glory

In 2009, for the first time after 39 years of being played at various global destinations, the year-end championship of men's professional tennis was held in London at the O2 Arena. London will remain the host city up until and including 2012.

In 1969 Jack Kramer, the first executive director of the Association of Tennis Professionals (ATP), implemented the Grand Prix structure of a year-long series of tennis tournaments. In 1970 the first Masters event was held in Tokyo and

was won by the American Stan Smith, the 1972 Wimbledon champion. Since then the year-end championships have been hosted around the world under several different names.

Initially called the Masters, the championships were held in Tokyo, Paris, Barcelona, Boston, Melbourne and Stockholm. Between 1977 and 1989 they were held in Madison Square Garden, New York. The list of winners there reads like a who's who of tennis.

In 1989 the championships were re-named the ATP World Tour Championships.

The German cities of Frankfurt and Hanover hosted the event from 1990 to 1999. In 2000 the event was re-named the Tennis Masters Cup and was played in Lisbon, Sydney, Shanghai and Houston. Australian Lleyton Hewitt grabbed the title two years running in 2001 and 2002. Roger Federer features prominently in the roll of honour.

The move to the O2 Arena in the heart of London was accompanied by another name change, to the ATP World Tour Finals. Despite the confusing change of names and venues the event remains

WHAT THE PLAYERS SAY ABOUT THE YEAR-END CHAMPIONSHIPS

❝ I would put it in the same league as a Grand Slam because the best eight players in the world are participating here. Certainly it says a lot about the quality, about the players who are playing here. It attracts attention from the tennis lovers and media worldwide. Everybody has a lot of motivation to end up the season in the best possible way. ❞
NOVAK DJOKOVIC

❝ The event has a great history and means so much to the top players. ❞
ANDY MURRAY

❝ This is one of the most important events and one of the most difficult to win since from day one you face a Top 10 player. No mistakes are allowed. ❞
RAFAEL NADAL

❝ Qualifying really shows that you've had a solid season, not just a good tournament or two. It's an event we certainly look forward to, and one that we get very motivated to play. ❞
BOB BRYAN, DOUBLES SPECIALIST

2005 year-end champion Argentine David Nalbandian

ROLL OF HONOUR

TENNIS MASTERS CUP

2008	SHANGHAI	**Novak Djokovic**
2007	SHANGHAI	**Roger Federer**
2006	SHANGHAI	**Roger Federer**
2005	SHANGHAI	**David Nalbandian**
2004	HOUSTON	**Roger Federer**
2003	HOUSTON	**Roger Federer**
2002	SHANGHAI	**Lleyton Hewitt**
2001	SYDNEY	**Lleyton Hewitt**
2000	LISBON	**Gustavo Kuerten**

ATP WORLD TOUR CHAMPIONSHIPS

1999	HANNOVER	**Pete Sampras**
1998	HANNOVER	**Alex Corretja**
1997	HANNOVER	**Pete Sampras**
1996	HANNOVER	**Pete Sampras**
1995	FRANKFURT	**Boris Becker**
1994	FRANKFURT	**Pete Sampras**
1993	FRANKFURT	**Michael Stich**
1992	FRANKFURT	**Boris Becker**
1991	FRANKFURT	**Pete Sampras**
1990	FRANKFURT	**Andre Agassi**

MASTERS

1989	NEW YORK	**Stefan Edberg**
1988	NEW YORK	**Boris Becker**
1987	NEW YORK	**Ivan Lendl**
1986	NEW YORK	**Ivan Lendl**
1985	NEW YORK	**Ivan Lendl**
1984	NEW YORK	**John McEnroe**
1983	NEW YORK	**John McEnroe**
1982	NEW YORK	**Ivan Lendl**
1981	NEW YORK	**Ivan Lendl**
1980	NEW YORK	**Bjorn Borg**
1979	NEW YORK	**Bjorn Borg**
1978	NEW YORK	**Brian Gottfried**
1977	NEW YORK	**Jimmy Connors**
1976	NEW YORK	**Manuel Orantes**
1975	STOCKHOLM	**Ilie Nastase**
1974	MELBOURNE	**Guillermo Vilas**
1973	BOSTON	**Ilie Nastase**
1972	BARCELONA	**Ilie Nastase**
1971	PARIS	**Ilie Nastase**
1970	TOKYO	**Stan Smith**

and has always been the year-end championships. After the Grand Slam events it is arguably the most important prize in tennis. Financially, it is one of the most lucrative. The prize money in 2009 was US$5 million.

The tournament's format is unique in tennis. The eight players that are selected to play in the event are the players who have accrued the most ranking points during the year.

These eight players are then split into two groups of four players for three round robin matches. There are two knockout semi-finals and one final to decide the winner.

This makes for some exceptional viewing for spectators. As Andy Murray says: "It's such a unique event. It's the only tournament where fans are guaranteed to see the top eight guys playing each other every day."

The eight-day tournament has a crowd capacity of just over 250,000 which makes it the biggest indoor tennis tournament of all time. For players and fans alike it has a unique appeal. ●

ATP BY NUMBERS

ATP World Tournaments in 2009	**62**
Singles players qualifying for the ATP World Tour Finals	**8**
ATP World Tour champion	**1**

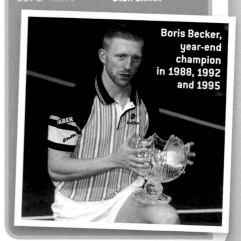

Boris Becker, year-end champion in 1988, 1992 and 1995

Kim Clijsters champion 2002 and 2003

Monica Seles, winner 1990-1992

Venus Williams, the 2008 Sony Ericsson champion

WTA TOUR CHAMPIONSHIPS

The season-ending women's championships are open to the top eight singles players of the year and the top four doubles pairs

Like the men's tour with its finale to the season, the women's tour reaches an end-of-year climax in November with a championship contested by the top eight players and the top four doubles pairs.

The first WTA Championships were held in 1972 in Boca Raton in Florida, USA,

following the foundation of the Women's Tennis Association (WTA) in 1970 by nine women players led by Billie Jean King. Owing to the fact that she was still classified as an amateur player, the champion, Chris Evert was unable to collect the US$25,000 winner's prize-money that year. In 2009 the total prize money was US$4.55 million, a reflection of how much the game has changed.

The WTA Championships have been sponsored by several companies and hosted in many cities. For 22 years between 1979 and 2000 they took place in New York at Madison Square Garden. The list of winners includes Martina Navratilova who won the Championships eight times.

Curiously she won twice in 1986, as due to a change of date the Championships

Gabriela Sabatini, the 1994 champion

DID YOU KNOW?

From 2011 until 2013 the Sony Ericsson Championships will be hosted in Istanbul, Turkey.

ROLL OF HONOUR

SONY ERICSSON CHAMPIONSHIPS

2008	DOHA	Venus Williams
2007	MADRID	Justine Henin
2006	MADRID	Justine Henin
2005	LOS ANGELES	Amelie Mauresmo

WTA TOUR CHAMPIONSHIPS

| 2004 | LOS ANGELES | Maria Sharapova |
| 2003 | LOS ANGELES | Kim Clijsters |

HOME DEPOT CHAMPIONSHIPS

| 2002 | LOS ANGELES | Kim Clijsters |

SANEX CHAMPIONSHIPS

| 2001 | MUNICH | Serena Williams |

CHASE CHAMPIONSHIPS

2000	NEW YORK	Martina Hingis
1999	NEW YORK	Lindsay Davenport
1998	NEW YORK	Martina Hingis
1997	NEW YORK	Jana Novotna
1996	NEW YORK	Steffi Graf

COREL CHAMPIONSHIPS

| 1995 | NEW YORK | Steffi Graf |

VIRGINIA SLIMS CHAMPIONSHIPS

1994	NEW YORK	Gabriela Sabatini
1993	NEW YORK	Steffi Graf
1992	NEW YORK	Monica Seles
1991	NEW YORK	Monica Seles
1990	NEW YORK	Monica Seles
1989	NEW YORK	Steffi Graf
1988	NEW YORK	Gabriela Sabatini
1987	NEW YORK	Steffi Graf
1986	NEW YORK	Martina Navratilova
1985	NEW YORK	Martina Navratilova
1984	NEW YORK	Martina Navratilova
1983	NEW YORK	Martina Navratilova

AVON CHAMPIONSHIPS

1982	NEW YORK	Sylvia Hanika
1981	NEW YORK	Martina Navratilova
1980	NEW YORK	Tracy Austin
1979	NEW YORK	Martina Navratilova

VIRGINIA SLIMS CHAMPIONSHIPS

1978	OAKLAND	Martina Navratilova
1977	NEW YORK	Chris Evert
1976	LOS ANGELES	Evonne Goolagong
1975	LOS ANGELES	Chris Evert
1974	LOS ANGELES	Evonne Goolagong
1973	BOCA RATON FL.	Chris Evert
1972	BOCA RATON FL.	Chris Evert

were staged twice: the first time in March and again in November. Steffi Graf claimed victory on five occasions. Her final year-end championship success was in 1996.

Since 2000 the Championships have been held in Munich, Los Angeles and Madrid, moving to their home at the Khalifa International Tennis Complex in Doha in 2008 to 2010. Then they move to Istanbul, Turkey, for three years until 2013.

The singles event begins as a round robin event with four players in each pool. Over the first four days of competition, each player meets the other three in their pool, with the top two in each pool moving on to the knockout semi-finals.

The first-placed player in one group meets the second-placed player in the other group and vice versa. The winners of each semi-final meet in the championship match.

The final is played over three sets, and it is interesting to note that between 1984

and 1998 the event featured a best of five set women's final. In 1990 Monica Seles, then a 16 year old, became the youngest champion when she beat Argentinian Gabriela Sabatini 6-4, 5-7, 3-6, 6-4, 6-2 in three hours and 47 minutes. This was the first WTA season-ending final to go five sets.

The doubles event, which features four teams, is a single elimination draw, beginning with the semi-final round.

After the four Grand Slam events, winning the WTA is the most coveted prize on the tour and the round robin format makes it a compelling event for spectators. ●

66 The event is a showcase for women's tennis 99

MARTINA NAVRATILOVA

Justine Henin, champion in 2006 and 2007 and making a comeback in 2010

TIM HENMAN

OLYMPIC TENNIS

Despite the riches and ranking points up for grabs on the Tour, winning an Olympic medal is one of the highlights of a player's career

2008 Olympic medallists: (left to right) Fernando Gonzalez, Rafael Nadal, Novak Djokovic

Elena Dementieva, gold medal, women's singles 2008

PETER NORFOLK

In 1896 at the Athens Olympics tennis was one of only nine sports that was represented. It remained an Olympic sport until 1924, after which a dispute between the International Tennis Federation (ITF) and the International Olympic Committee (IOC) kept tennis out of the games.

In 1968 tennis was included in the Olympic games in Mexico, although only as a demonstration sport. In 1984 tennis was an under-21 year old demonstration event in Los Angeles.

It was not until 1988 in Seoul, South Korea, that tennis was restored as an Olympic sport. Its inclusion paved the way for other professional athletes to be included in the games.

Germany's Steffi Graf picked up the gold medal in the women's singles in 1988 defeating Argentina's Gabriela Sabatini 6-3 6-3 in the final. In so doing the German was on her way to achieving the "Golden Slam". That year Graf won each of the four Slams in addition to her gold medal. No other player in history has achieved such a feat.

The format of Olympic tennis is a conventional tournament with a 64 draw for singles and a 32 draw for doubles. Each country has a maximum of six men and six women that can play and only four of those can compete in each singles event with a maximum of two doubles teams in each doubles event.

In 2008 rankings points were awarded for the event with a men's gold medal worth 400 points and a women's gold medal worth 353 WTA ranking points.

Many of the sport's biggest names have won medals at the games, from the 2000 singles champions Venus Williams and Yevgeny Kafelnikov to Rafael Nadal, Andre Agassi, Gabriela Sabatini, Arantxa Sanchez Vicario and Serena Williams.

Wheelchair tennis was introduced to the Paralympic Games in 1988 as a demonstration sport and achieved full medal status in 1992 at Barcelona. It remains one of the highest-profile events in the Paralympic Games and in September 2008 all of the top players competed.

Britain's Peter Norfolk won the gold medal in Beijing successfully defending the Quad singles title he had won in 2004 in Athens when quadraplegics were able to participate in singles and doubles competitions for the first time. Norfolk also won a bronze medal with Jamie Burdekin in the quad doubles.

At the 2008 Olympics in Beijing, the Russian Elena Dementieva won the women's singles and she summed up how it felt. "It's very difficult to explain the way I feel right now. It takes I think a few days before I realize I'm Olympic champion. But this is, for sure, the biggest moment in my career, in my life. I will never forget this moment," she said.

Perhaps the mighty Roger Federer best explains the importance of the Olympic Games in the tennis calendar. In 2008, the man who is arguably the greatest tennis player of all time won Olympic gold with his fellow Swiss player and friend Stanislas Wawrinka. In the men's doubles event they defeated Sweden's Simon Aspelin and Thomas Johansson 6-3 6-4 6-7 (4) 6-3.

It was Federer's third attempt at winning a medal. The great man said: "The joy of sharing this victory with somebody else who I like very much, who we had a great two weeks with, it's quite different to anything I've ever gone through. I could only maybe compare it a little bit to some incredible Davis Cup victories I've ever had." ●

> **❝ It takes I think a few days before I realize I'm Olympic champion. But this is, for sure, the biggest moment in my career, in my life. I will never forget this moment. ❞**
>
> ELENA DEMENTIEVA, GOLD MEDALLIST, BEIJING 2008

ROLL OF HONOUR
2008 BEIJING, CHINA

MEN'S SINGLES

Gold	Rafael Nadal (ESP)
Silver	Fernando Gonzalez (CHI)
Bronze	Novak Djokovic (SRB)

WOMEN'S SINGLES

Gold	Elena Dementieva (RUS)
Silver	Dinara Safina (RUS)
Bronze	Vera Zvonareva (RUS)

MEN'S DOUBLES

Gold	Roger Federer and Stanislas Wawrinka (SUI)
Silver	Simon Aspelin and Thomas Johansson (SWE)
Bronze	Bob and Mike Bryan (USA)

WOMEN'S DOUBLES

Gold	Serena and Venus Williams (USA)
Silver	Medina and Ruano (ESP)
Bronze	Yan Zi and Zheng Jie (CHI)

ROLL OF HONOUR
2004 ATHENS, GREECE

MEN'S SINGLES

Gold	Nicolas Massu (CHI)
Silver	Mardy Fish (USA)
Bronze	Fernando Gonzalez (CHI)

WOMEN'S SINGLES

Gold	Justine Henin (BEL)
Silver	Amelie Mauresmo (FRA)
Bronze	Alicia Molik (AUS)

ROLL OF HONOUR
2000 SYDNEY, AUSTRALIA

MEN'S SINGLES

Gold	Yevgeny Kafelnikov (RUS)
Silver	Tommy Haas (GER)
Bronze	Arnaud DiPasquale (FRA)

WOMEN'S SINGLES

Gold	Venus Williams (USA)
Silver	Elena Dementieva (RUS)
Bronze	Monica Seles (USA)

Venus Williams USA flag bearer, Sydney 2000

THE DAVIS CUP

DAVIS CUP

In little over 100 years, what started as the brainchild of a Harvard graduate has developed into the largest annual international team competition in world sport

The Spanish team celebrates Davis Cup victory in 2008, defeating Argentina in the final

American tennis player Dwight Filley Davis conceived and co-founded the International Lawn Tennis Challenge in 1899 so that his Harvard University tennis team could challenge a team from Great Britain, and donated a silver bowl to be awarded to the winners of the first competition a year later. As a result, the "Challenge" was renamed the Davis Cup thereafter.

For the first three years, only Great Britain and the USA competed, but the format soon lead to interest from other

FORMAT

Davis Cup ties consist of five matches, or rubbers, played over three days from Friday to Sunday. The captain nominates a squad of four players and selects his first two singles players. The order of play for the first day is then drawn at random.

Two singles rubbers are played on Friday, the doubles on Saturday and the two 'reverse' singles on Sunday, so-called as players play the opponent they didn't face on Friday, although substitutions are allowed. A team must win three rubbers to seal a tie.

'Live' rubbers – that can affect the outcome of the tie – are over five sets with no tie-break in the fifth set, while 'dead' rubbers are three tie-break sets.

Andy Murray and Ross Hutchins represent Great Britain in the doubles

The first USA team: (from left to right) Malcolm Whitman, Dwight F. Davis, and Holcombe Ward

DAVIS CUP WINNERS

2008: Spain defeated Argentina
2007: USA defeated Russia
2006: Russia defeated Argentina
2005: Croatia defeated Slovakia

LEGENDS

Nicola Pietrangeli is widely regarded as the greatest Davis Cup player of all time. The Italian played 164 rubbers for his country between 1954 and 1972, winning a record 120 matches. He helped Italy reach consecutive Davis Cup finals in 1960 and 1961, losing both to an Australian team featuring Rod Laver, Roy Emerson and Neale Fraser. After retiring, Pietrangeli captained the nation to its only Davis Cup title in 1976.

The Four Musketeers Rene Lacoste, Henri Cochet, Jean Borotra and Jacques Brugnon claimed France's first ever Davis Cup victory in 1927, and retained the trophy for the next six years in a golden era in French tennis.

John McEnroe will forever be remembered as the "Superbrat" of tennis, but was also a dedicated member of the US Davis Cup team for 12 years. A member of five victorious squads, he once famously declared: "I will go anywhere, anytime to play Davis Cup for America." His brother Patrick captains the current Davis Cup team.

RECORDS

Most successful nation: USA – 32 Davis Cup titles
Most successful player: Roy Emerson (Australia) – 8 Davis Cup titles
Longest match: 1982 World Group quarter-final: John McEnroe (USA) beat Mats Wilander (Sweden) 9-7 6-2 15-17 3-6 8-6. The match lasted 6hrs 22mins.
Oldest player: Yaka-Garonfin Koptigan (Togo) – 59yrs 147 days
Youngest player: Mohammed-Akhtar Hossain (Bangladesh) – 13yrs 326 days
Record attendance: 27,200 at the Estadio Olimpico in Seville for the 2004 Davis Cup final between Spain and USA

> ❝ 131 nations entered the 2009 Davis Cup, making it the largest annual international team sports competition in the world ❞

nations. France and Australasia (Australia and New Zealand, who played together until 1914) soon entered the competition, which gradually grew and grew. Fifty nations were involved by 1969, but the competition was dominated by the four founding nations until 1973. This is partially responsible for the location of the four Grand Slams.

All that changed in 1974 when South Africa and India reached the final. The Indian team withdrew in protest against the South African government's apartheid policy, handing South Africa victory. To date, South Africa has never contested a Davis Cup final.

The competition has always drawn the biggest names in men's tennis. In the history of the competition the likes of Fred Perry, Rod Laver, Bjorn Borg, John McEnroe, Pete Sampras and Rafael Nadal have played prominent roles in Davis Cup victories for their countries.

In 1993, a hundred nations entered the competition, which by then had been adapted to split the entrants into continental 'zones', each aiming to reach the elite World Group of 16 nations who compete for the Davis Cup title each year. To date 12 different national teams have now won the competition with the USA the most successful team in history.

A total of 131 nations entered the 2009 Davis Cup, making it the largest annual international team sports competition in the world. To this day, more than a century since its inception, ties are still played in the original three-day format that Dwight Filley Davis and his Harvard teammates devised back in 1899. ●

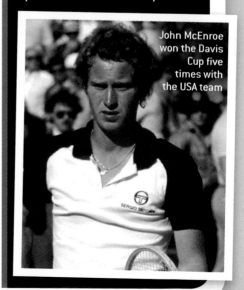

John McEnroe won the Davis Cup five times with the USA team

FED CUP

The entry list has grown, the format has evolved, the name has changed but Mrs Wightman's vision of a premier team tennis competition for women endures

Over 40 years after Mrs Hotchkiss Wightman first proposed an international team tennis event for women back in 1919 and following the continued efforts of Nell Hopman and Mary Hardwick Hare, the International Tennis Federation marked its 50th anniversary by launching the Federation Cup in 1963. This was a one-week national team competition played at a different venue each year.

The format was slightly different to the three-day men's competitions known as the Davis Cup, as it had three rubbers (a term for a singles or doubles match in

FORMAT

Teams in World Groups I and II play five-rubber (singles or doubles matches) knockout ties over three weekends in the year to crown the Fed Cup champions. First-round losers from World Group I play off against first-round winners from World Group II to determine their standing for the following year's competition. First-round losers from World Group II play off against the champions of the Zonal Groups from the Americas and Asia/Oceania, and two teams from the Europe/Africa Zone.

Outside the World Groups, ties are the traditional three-rubbers — two singles and a doubles completed in a day.

TIE is the name given to the event. **RUBBER** is the name given to each of the matches contained within the tie.

Kateryna Bondarenko in Fed Cup action for the Ukrainian team

RECORDS

Most successful nation:
USA — 17 Fed Cup titles

Most successful captains:
Vicky Berner (USA), Billie Jean King (USA) and Miguel Margets (Spain) — 4 titles each

Most rubbers played:
Arantxa Sanchez Vicario (Spain) — 100

Youngest player: Denise Panagopoulou (Greece) — 12 years 360 days

Oldest player:
Gill Butterfield (Bermuda) — 52 years 162 days

Most games in a rubber:
54 — Nathalie Tauziat (France) beat Naoko Sawamatsu (Japan) 7-5 4-6 17-15, 1997 World Group 1st round

Elena Dementieva is Russia's most successful Fed Cup player and almost single-handedly beat France in 2005

ARANTXA SANCHEZ-VICARIO

STAR SPANGLED WINNERS

The golden era of US Fed Cup tennis fell between 1976 and 1982. The team won seven consecutive crowns, winning 37 consecutive ties and a staggering 64 consecutive rubbers (matches) along the way.

The biggest names in American tennis have each left their mark on the nation's Fed Cup legacy. King won five titles as a player and four as a captain. Chris Evert posted the longest winning streak in the event's history with 29 undefeated singles rubbers between 1977 and 1986, while Martina Navratilova — who first played Fed Cup for Czechoslovakia — won 40 rubbers during her 29-year career before losing her one and only rubber in her last tie in 2004, aged 47.

> **Aided by the some of the biggest names in the women's game, the competition had proved to be a great success**

team competitions, see box) allowing the event to be completed in a day.

The inaugural competition was played at Queen's Club in west London. Despite the fact that there was no prize money on offer and teams had to pay to compete, 16 nations contested for the honour of being hailed as the first Federation Cup champions.

The final featured tennis superpowers Australia and the United States. Australian legend Margaret Court played against US tennis visionary Billie Jean King. The United States team emerged victorious — the first of 17 titles to head to America.

Aided by the support of some of the biggest names in the women's game, the competition proved to be a great success and continued in its one-week format until 1994. By then, 73 nations had entered the competition, which meant that host nations were required to construct purpose-built tennis facilities in order to stage the competition. The boost to each host nation's tennis infrastructure became a part of the legacy of the competition.

In 1995 the Federation Cup adopted a new format and abbreviated its name to the Fed Cup. In recognition of the atmosphere and prestige of players representing their home country in front of their home crowd, the Fed Cup introduced home and away ties similar to those played in Davis Cup competition. Over the next decade a number of adjustments were made to the competition format until in 2005 a two-tier World Group was established, splitting the leading 16 nations into two groups of eight.

Today over 80 countries enter the Fed Cup each year, with many of the world's top female players representing their nations. Among those flying the flag with pride around the world are the Williams sisters, Serena and Venus, Ana Ivanovic, Maria Sharapova and Dinara Safina. ●

American legend Chris Evert won 29 consecutive Fed Cup matches for the US

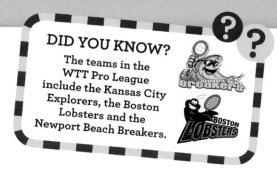

TEAM TENNIS

There's a lot more to tennis than just singles and doubles tournaments

Mark Philippoussis is held aloft by his teammates after Australia's Davis Cup victory over France in 1999

AUSTRALIAN DAVIS CUP TEAM 1999

66 Tennis has sort of evolved thanks to World TeamTennis. Most of all, what I like about it is the equality of the genders, where men and women are treated the same way and they can contribute the same way 99

MARTINA NAVRATILOVA

Team GB celebrates Andy Murray's Davis Cup singles rubber victory

UKRAINIAN FED CUP TEAM 2008

WORLD TEAM TENNIS INNOVATIONS

Over the years, the WTT Pro League has pioneered a number of rule changes and technologies now present on the ATP and WTA Tours:

- Multi-coloured hard court surfaces, adopted by the Australian and US Open tournament organisers, have been a feature of World Team Tennis since 1973.

- The deciding "supertiebreaker", a WTT innovation, has now replaced the third set in doubles matches in the majority of ATP and WTA tournaments.

- On-court coaching, instant replay technology and the challenge system all started life in the WTT.

"MR HOPMAN"

Few people have demonstrated a greater lifelong love for tennis than Harry Hopman. The Australian was a successful doubles specialist, winning seven Grand Slam titles. His greatest achievements came as captain of the Australian Davis Cup team. Hopman captained his country to 15 Davis Cup titles and a further five finals before emigrating to the United States to establish his first tennis academy.

Such was the respect for his achievements and knowledge of the sport that the players at his academies always addressed him as "Mr Hopman". Four years after his death in 1985 at the age of 79, former academy player and fellow Australian Paul McNamee founded the season-opening Hopman Cup in his honour, attended each year by his widow and "Queen of the Cup", Lucy Hopman.

Dominik Hrbaty (left) and Dominika Cibulkova of the Slovak Republic with Lucy Hopman in 2009

Although a very social pastime, the game of tennis is often described as a solitary pursuit, as players – or pairs in doubles – face off against one another for their own personal glory. But there are a number of competitions in which tennis is played as a team sport.

Team tennis is nearly as old as the modern game itself, dating back to the turn of the 20th century when the Davis Cup (see page 46) first allowed four-man male squads to represent their country. With each match worth one point, or 'rubber', the five-match ties – four singles and one doubles – played over three days proved to be such a hit that the format has remained unchanged since Great Britain and the United States competed the first tie back in 1899.

Today, players of all ages and abilities can get involved in team tennis. Many players enjoy the camaraderie and support that comes with playing in a team, while others relish the chance to represent their club, school, university, county, and even their nation in league and cup competitions across the globe. There is a certain buzz in the air for both fans and players when there is more at stake than just the personal fortunes of a single player.

And while the Davis Cup has grown to become one of the most prestigious international accolades in world sport, further international team tennis events have emerged. Its sister competition, the Fed Cup (see page 48), has offered female players the chance to play for their country since 1963, with both popular competitions running throughout the tennis season as ties are scheduled between top-flight tournaments.

However, the Fed Cup began life as a one-week competition, and such team events still exist today. The ATP launched the World Team Cup in 1978, inviting the eight nations whose top two players' combined rankings are highest to compete on the clay courts of the Rochusclub in Dusseldorf shortly before the French Open. In Perth, Western Australia, mixed doubles pairs from around the globe are invited to play at the Hopman Cup, the premier international mixed doubles competition. It was founded in 1989 and named after legendary Australian tennis player and coach Harry Hopman.

Team tennis stretches beyond gender equality as well. Each summer in the United States, juniors, veterans, and touring professionals from around the world compete side-by-side in the World Team Tennis Pro League, representing franchises from cities across the country. The competition is popular with players and fans because professionals and amateurs play together in teams and there is a chance to see rising stars play alongside the legends of the game. ●

> What sets Federer apart is his ability to make the game of tennis beautiful to behold

PROFILE

Roger Federer
8 August 1981
Basel, Switzerland
6' 1" (185cm)
187lbs (85kg)
Right-handed, one-handed backhand
1998
www.rogerfederer.com

DID YOU KNOW?
At the 2009 US Open, Federer played a through-the-legs cross-court pass that flew beyond Novak Djokovic to bring up match point in their semi-final clash. He later described it as the greatest shot of his career.

ROGER FEDERER

Wimbledon 2009

Roland Garros 2009

HISTORY BOOK

- CAREER SINGLES TITLES: **61**
- GRAND SLAM SINGLES TITLES: **15**
- GRAND SLAM SINGLES RECORD

Australian Open:	2007, 2006, 2004
Roland Garros:	2009
Wimbledon:	2009, 2007, 2006, 2005, 2004, 2003
US Open:	2008, 2007, 2006, 2005, 2004

The most successful player of his generation, Roger Federer has set a new standard for tennis

R oger Federer will be remembered as one of the greatest sportsmen of all time. The Swiss has won more Grand Slams in the Open era than any other men's tennis player, posting victories at all four Slams, and once holding the world No.1 ranking for a record 237 consecutive weeks. But what truly sets Federer apart is his ability to make the game of tennis beautiful to behold.

The poise and dynamism of Federer's movement is often compared to that of a ballet dancer – rarely is he rushed or off-balance, a skill that allows him to play tennis that at times stretches beyond the imaginations of his fellow professionals.

While Federer's serve does not possess raw pace, both his first and second serves are hit with great accuracy and disguise. His forehand and backhand drives are played with a smooth motion that requires incredible timing, but which delivers pace, spin and subtle touch. His slice backhand, a defensive stroke for most players, is regarded as a weapon. When forced to defend, Federer has left opponents stunned with improvised squash-like sliced drives, smashed lobs and impossibly angled passing shots.

All this is a far cry from the short-tempered junior whose embarrassing behaviour prompted his parents to threaten to stop driving him to tournaments. Aged three he showed precocious talent after first picking up a racket at his local tennis club. "I knew what I could do and failure made me mad," he remembers. "I had two voices inside me, the devil and the angel. 'How could you miss that?' one voice would say. Then I would just explode."

In the summer of 2002, a year after Federer had ended his idol Pete Sampras' 31-match unbeaten run at Wimbledon, Peter Carter, his first coach, died in a car crash. "He is the one person who truly opened my eyes to what I could achieve, because maybe I was not taking the game seriously enough at times."

It changed Federer's perspective on tennis and he developed a ruthless focus. When he claimed the first of five consecutive Wimbledon titles in 2003, he dedicated his victory to Carter. "Whenever I win, particularly big matches, I'm thinking of him for sure."

The following year was a landmark one for Federer. He claimed three of the four Slams and rose to world No.1 after winning the Australian Open. He defended his Wimbledon title and won his first US Open title. Since Wimbledon of that year, Federer has reached the semi-finals of every Grand Slam event to date.

A year later he ended the season with 82 wins and just three defeats as he defended both his Wimbledon and US Open crowns. In both 2006 and 2007 he again won three of the four Slams, with only the French Open eluding him as Rafael Nadal proved to be Federer's undoing on a clay court. The Spaniard emerged as Federer's closest rival, and in 2008 ended the Swiss' five-year dominance at Wimbledon in a five-set match regarded as one of the greatest matches of all time, before later replacing Federer as world No.1.

Federer completed his career Grand Slam with victory at Roland Garros in 2009, before winning a sixth Wimbledon crown and a record 15th Grand Slam title, which returned him to the top of the world rankings. Juan Martin del Potro later ended his winning streak at the US Open in five sets.

Now a father of twin daughters, Charlene and Myla, Federer is entering the final years of an incredible career. Along with Nadal, there are challengers emerging who are intent on ending his era of dominance, but when he does call time on his career he will be remembered as the man who single-handedly raised the bar for modern tennis. ●

STATS AMAZING

In Grand Slam tournaments from 2004 until 2009 Federer won 124 consecutive matches against players ranked outside of the world's top five. At the 2009 US Open, world No.6 Juan Martin del Potro ended the streak in the final. The Argentine was ranked No.5 by the end of the tournament.

RAFAEL NADAL

Left-handed Nadal puts all
his strength into a shot

PROFILE

Rafael Nadal
3 June 2006
Manacor, Mallorca, Spain
6'1" (185cms)
160lbs (72kg)
Right-handed, two-handed backhand
2001
www.rafaelnadal.com

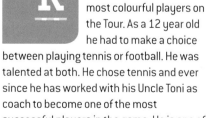

STATS AMAZING

When Rafa won at Roland Garros in
2005 it was the first time he had played
at the French Open.

The hard-working Mallorcan has a big game that has taken him to the top of the rankings

R afael Nadal, or Rafa as he is known, is one of the most colourful players on the Tour. As a 12 year old he had to make a choice between playing tennis or football. He was talented at both. He chose tennis and ever since he has worked with his Uncle Toni as coach to become one of the most successful players in the game. He is one of only nine players in the modern era to win a main Tour victory before the age of 16.

He plays left-handed, although he is actually right-handed in everything else.

(He's right-footed when it comes to football.) Rafa started playing tennis when he was four years old. At the age of nine he had a two-handed forehand and backhand, but he now plays a double-handed backhand and single- handed forehand.

He was a star at an early age; winning his first ATP victory at the age of 15 when he beat the Uruguayan player Ramon Delgado, then ranked 81 in the world. At that time his ranking was 762. That was the start of an incredible story.

In 2003 as a 17 year old he played two Grand Slam events, reaching the third round of Wimbledon, and finished the end of the year in the Top 50 – very impressive for a young man who could still have been playing junior events.

He was only 17 years and eight months old when he made his Davis Cup debut and helped secure victory for Spain over the Czech Republic.

Growing up on clay courts in Mallorca, Spain, it is not surprising that this has proved to be Rafa's most successful surface. He won his first Grand Slam title at Roland Garros in 2005, the first time he had ever entered the event. He then went on to win the French Open three more consecutive times, equaling the record of Bjorn Borg (1978–1981). Like Borg, he also managed back-to-back French Open and Wimbledon victories in 2008. He beat Roger Federer in an epic Wimbledon final.

The win at Wimbledon was significant because it propelled Rafa to the No.1 world ranking. It also demonstrated that the 6ft 1in Spaniard had managed to adapt his game from his natural aggressive baseline play, which was so effective on the red clay, to a more varied game that brought victory

on grass. He defeated Roger Federer, a player who is considered to be one of the best ever grass-court players.

Off court Rafa remains down to earth. He still has plenty of time for his fans. At an autograph session in Rome in 2005 he spent more time than scheduled signing autographs and when one of his fans was knocked over in the rush to reach him, Rafa invited the fan to sit with him while he finished signing the autographs.

66 I consider myself lucky to work in something that I love 99

Nadal has great respect for his fellow players. At the end of a Davis Cup match against France, in Alicante in September 2004, having shaken the hand of his opponent Arnaud Clement, the team captain Guy Forget and the umpire as is expected, Rafa then shook hands with each member of the French team. Afterwards he said that he had decided to do this whatever the outcome of the tie as "I have enormous

respect both for the players and for the competition". A sense of fair play shines through Nadal's tennis on and off court.

The Rafa Nadal Foundation was created in February 2008 and it aims to promote integration and tolerance through the sport. Nadal's family with assistance from Carlos Costa, the former player and now his agent, run the Foundation. "I'm happy to have created my foundation and to be able to raise funds which will contribute towards helping people in need," Nadal said. "I consider myself lucky to be able to work in something I love."

With his colourful clothes and his down to earth manner, Nadal remains one of the most respected players on the Tour, as well as one of the best. ●

HISTORY BOOK

- **CAREER SINGLES TITLES: 62**
- **GRAND SLAM SINGLES TITLES: 6**
- **GRAND SLAM SINGLES RECORD**

Australian Open:	2009
Roland Garros:	2005, 2006, 2007, 2008
Wimbledon:	2008
US Open:	Semi-Final 2008

Nadal with fellow tennis player and friend Feliciano Lopez

?? DID YOU KNOW?
Rafa's other uncle Miguel Angel Nadal is a former professional soccer player who played for FC Barcelona, Real Mallorca and the Spanish national team.

Rafa tastes victory with the Wimbledon trophy in 2008

PLAYER **PROFILE**

> Murray is one of the best tacticians in the game and along with his all-round game is a feared competitor on the Tour

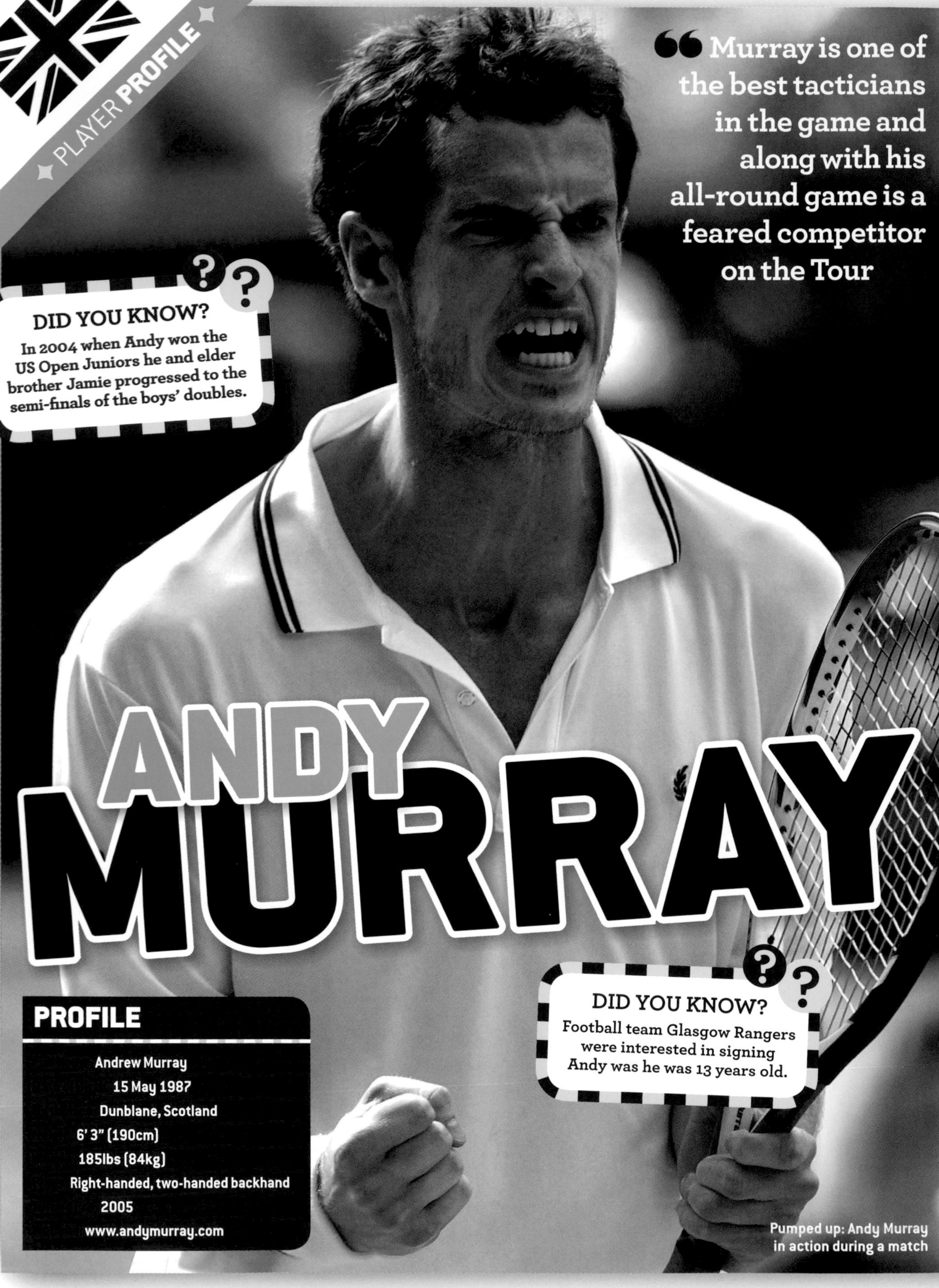

ANDY MURRAY

DID YOU KNOW?

In 2004 when Andy won the US Open Juniors he and elder brother Jamie progressed to the semi-finals of the boys' doubles.

PROFILE

Andrew Murray
15 May 1987
Dunblane, Scotland
6' 3" (190cm)
185lbs (84kg)
Right-handed, two-handed backhand
2005
www.andymurray.com

DID YOU KNOW?

Football team Glasgow Rangers were interested in signing Andy was he was 13 years old.

Pumped up: Andy Murray in action during a match

JAMIE MURRAY

Agony or ecstasy?
Murray roars at Wimbledon

DID YOU KNOW?

In August 2009 Murray was ranked No.2 in the world.

HISTORY BOOK

- CAREER SINGLES TITLES: 13
- GRAND SLAM SINGLES TITLES: 0
- GRAND SLAM SINGLES RECORD

Australian Open:	Fourth Round 2009
Roland Garros:	Quarter-Final 2009
Wimbledon:	Semi-Final 2009
US Open:	Final 2008

Murray has sport in his genes. His grandfather was a professional footballer for Hibernian and his mother, Judy, is a well-respected tennis coach

Murray was born in Dunblane in Scotland the second of two sons. Brother Jamie was already 15 months old when Andy arrived. Both play tennis. Jamie has become a doubles specialist and as kids growing up they used to hit together. In the early days Jamie used to beat Andy until they played an under 10 event in Solihull and Andy won 7-6 6-3.

Andy has commented that his rivalry with Jamie may be one of the reasons he has achieved so much: "although it's good to learn how to win, it's almost better to learn from defeat, and I think my brother was a huge reason why I'm doing well just now," he said in 2006.

A prodigious talent, aged 12 Andy won the prestigious Orange Bowl Trophy. A year later he thought he was tired of tennis and joined the local football club where his talent was spotted by Glasgow Rangers scouts who wanted to sign him. Murray quickly returned to tennis realising that he loved the one-to-one combat.

At 15 years old, inspired by the fact that he had seen Rafael Nadal, only one year older than him, hitting with former world No.2 Carlos Moya, and that perhaps hitting with Jamie was never going to allow him to realise his ambition, Murray left Scotland to attend the Sanchez Casal Academy in Barcelona. Two years later in September 2004 he won the US Open Junior boys event.

In 2005 Murray turned pro and made his Davis Cup debut becoming the youngest man to represent GB in the tie against Israel in Tel Aviv where, partnering David Sherwood, he pulled off a superb doubles victory against the seasoned pair of Jonathan Erlich and Andy Ram.

On the international stage the marker was also put firmly down. Andy reached the final of an ATP Tour event in only his eighth event, testament to how quickly his talent had grown. In 2006 he won his first Tour event in San Jose and became the fourth youngest player ever to win that event.

He also broke into the top 50 for the first time. Only Borg, Hewitt, Nadal and Roddick were younger when they cracked the top 50. In Cincinnati he scored a victory over world No.1 Roger Federer, to become only the second man (along with Nadal) to beat Federer that year.

Murray has the honour of recording one of the most devastating wins in the first round of the 2007 Australian Open when he beat Spain's Alberto Martin with the loss of one game. He went on to lose to Nadal in the fourth round in a five-set match. A wrist injury sustained in Hamburg left him out of action for four months of the year but despite this Murray still ended the year in the top 15. In 2008 he reached the top 10 and won five ATP titles, including his first Masters event at Cincinnati, and in August 2009 he became the world No.2.

Murray is one of the best tacticians in the game and along with his all-round game is a feared competitor on the Tour. In their first nine meetings, Murray beat Federer six times. Murray's return of serve is considered to be one of the best in the game. Coached in the early days by Mark Petchey, now a TV commentator, and then high-profile American Brad Gilbert, Murray now has a team to assist him in his game.

Team Murray is a unique concept in the game. It means that Murray travels with a team rather than one coach. Murray's approach to his technical development and his physical improvements have propelled him to the top of his game.

He quickly assumed the mantle of British No.1 but his eyes are firmly focused on the world rankings where he has already proven he is one of the best players in the world. ●

Murray playing for Great Britain in a Davis Cup tie

2008 Australian Open champion

NOVAK DJOKOVIC

Serbian Novak Djokovic is one of the best players currently on the Tour, not to mention one of the most entertaining

The eldest of three brothers, Djokovic spent his school holidays at the mountain resort of Kapaonik, where his parents owned a restaurant and ran skiing lessons in the winter. "My father played football and was a skier," said Djokovic. "And my mother trained in sports. But nobody in my family ever played tennis. They were completely unfamiliar with the sport."

That all changed when Djokovic was four years old. Three tennis courts were built opposite the family restaurant and young Novak began taking lessons. "It was my destiny to play this sport," he believes. "I loved it from the start and really dedicated myself to it."

Djokovic was just 11 years old when the Kosovo War ravaged his hometown of Belgrade. For two months in 1999 the city was bombed every night, forcing the family to move from one building to

PROFILE

Novak Djokovic
22 May 1987
Belgrade, Serbia
6' 1" (187cm)
176lbs (80kg)
Right-handed, two-handed backhand
2003
www.novakdjokovic.rs

another in search of shelter. That summer, his parents sent him to the Nikola Pilic tennis academy in Munich, Germany, where he spent the next two years.

Away from the conflict, Djokovic had to come to terms with being uprooted from his family. His parents worked tirelessly in the family restaurant to pay for his tuition and travel to junior tournaments across Europe. It was a painful period in Novak's life, but the mental strength gained from such hardship has served him well during his career.

The Serb does not possess a signature weapon in his all-court game but his fleet-footed movement and defensive skills are twinned with the double threat of his booming forehand and backhand. "I'm a

A moment of contemplation in a match

Celebrating on the grass

DID YOU KNOW?

The Djokovic family hosts and runs the Serbia Open, the first ATP tournament to be played in the country, in Novak's home town of Belgrade. His uncle Goran is the tournament director.

HISTORY BOOK

- CAREER SINGLES TITLES: 13
- GRAND SLAM SINGLES TITLES: 1

- GRAND SLAM SINGLES RECORD

Australian Open:	2008
Roland Garros:	Semi-Final 2008, 2007
Wimbledon:	Semi-Final 2007
US Open:	Final 2007

STATS AMAZING

Novak Djokovic is the youngest player to reach the semi-finals of all four Grand Slams in the Open era; completing the set at the 2008 Australian Open aged 20 years 247 days.

> ❝ It was my destiny to play this sport – I loved it from the start and really dedicated myself to it ❞

groundstroke player and I play pretty aggressive," Djokovic says, "I like the fast rallies, I try to be pretty fast on the court."

After turning professional aged 16, Djokovic broke into the world's top 10 in 2007 following back-to-back Masters Series final appearances at Indian Wells and Miami before reaching the semi-finals at Roland Garros and Wimbledon. Djokovic lost both to Rafael Nadal, retiring from the Wimbledon semi-final after winning a grueling five-hour quarter-final against Marcos Baghdatis. In September he went one better in New York, reaching his first Grand Slam final at the US Open where he lost to defending champion Roger Federer.

Having finished the year ranked No.3 in the world, Djokovic ended Federer's streak of ten consecutive Grand Slam final appearances in the semi-finals of the 2008 Australian Open. Facing Jo-Wilfried Tsonga in the final, the 20 year old claimed his first Grand Slam title. Later that year Djokovic took the bronze medal at the Beijing Olympics and won the season-ending ATP World Tour Finals.

An established top-five player by the age of 21, Djokovic is renowned for his impersonations of fellow players. After his 2007 US Open quarter-final win against Carlos Moya, Djokovic treated the New York crowd to impressions of Rafael Nadal and Maria Sharapova, adjusting his clothes and mimicking their warm-up habits, routines between points and service actions.

At the 2009 US Open he mimicked tennis legend John McEnroe, who came down courtside from the commentary box to impersonate Djokovic himself, mocking the Serb's habit for bouncing the ball incessantly before serving.

Despite the showman reputation, Djokovic insists he is simply enjoying a life that might never have been, given the political and economic challenges he and his family have overcome: "Tennis hopefully is going to be my life for the next 10, 15 years, so you have to take it more or less in a positive way, and take everything with a smile – bring out the positive energy, make the people laugh, enjoy yourself. That's what I'm doing." ●

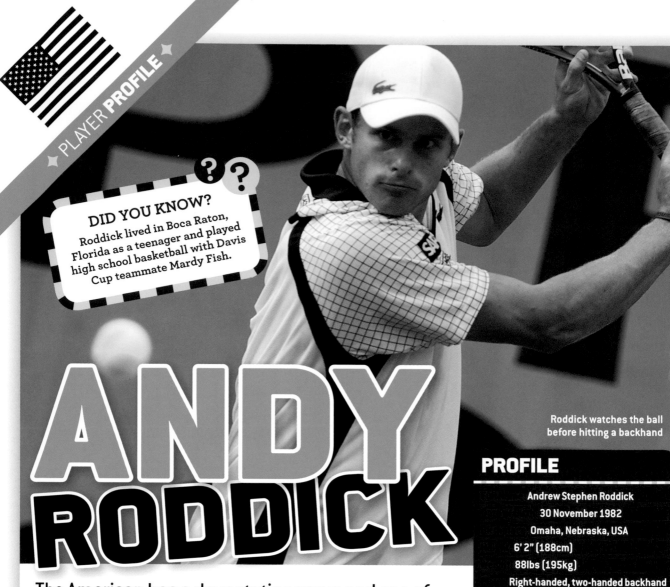

DID YOU KNOW?
Roddick lived in Boca Raton, Florida as a teenager and played high school basketball with Davis Cup teammate Mardy Fish.

Roddick watches the ball before hitting a backhand

ANDY RODDICK

The American has a devastating serve and one of the most impressive Davis Cup records in the game

PROFILE

Andrew Stephen Roddick
30 November 1982
Omaha, Nebraska, USA
6' 2" (188cm)
88lbs (195kg)
Right-handed, two-handed backhand
2000
www.andyroddick.com

The youngest of three tennis-playing brothers, Andy Roddick has never been short on confidence. After his first visit to Flushing Meadows to watch the US Open from the stands in 1991, he gave each member of his family a signed tennis ball and said, "hold on to this – it might be valuable one day."

Twelve years later, the nine-year-old from Nebraska's bold prediction came true. Just days after his 21st birthday, Roddick clinched the 2003 US Open title, beating Juan Carlos Ferrero 6-3, 7-6, 6-3 in the final, and shortly after replaced Ferrero as the world No.1. The result confirmed his status as the flag-bearer

for the next generation of American men's tennis players as Roddick, James Blake, Mardy Fish and the Bryan brothers emerged from the shadows of Pete Sampras, Andre Agassi, Jim Courier and Michael Chang.

Roddick's serve is by far his most devastating stroke. He has an abbreviated technique discovered almost by accident when he was messing around with friends to see who could hit the

STATS AMAZING !

Andy Roddick has won at least one ATP title every year since 2001, a record he shares with Roger Federer.

hardest serve. Rather than swinging the racket behind his head as the vast majority of players do, Roddick raises both arms upwards together and quickly bends his knees before rapidly uncoiling with incredible force. Roddick hit the fastest serve of all time, recorded at 155mph (249.5km/h), during the 2004 Davis Cup semi-final against Vladimir Voltchkov of Belarus.

To date his 2003 US Open triumph remains his only major title, but few consider Roddick to be a one-Slam wonder. Since then, the American has reached a further four Grand Slam finals – three at Wimbledon and a further US Open final appearance – losing each of them to Roger Federer, the man who

DID YOU KNOW?
Andy shares his 'A-Rod' nickname with Major League Baseball superstar Alex Rodriguez.

On the grass at Wimbledon chasing the low bouncing ball

HISTORY BOOK

- **CAREER SINGLES TITLES: 27**
- **GRAND SLAM SINGLES TITLES: 1**
- **GRAND SLAM SINGLES RECORD**

Australian Open:	Semi-Final 2003, Semi-Final 2005, Semi-Final 2007, Semi-Final 2009
Roland Garros:	Fourth Round 2009
Wimbledon:	Final 2004, 2005, 2009
US Open:	2003

Celebrating victory in Doha

DID YOU KNOW?
Andy always wears a blue Andy Roddick Foundation wristband, inscribed with the phrase 'No Compromise'.

replaced him as world No.1 in 2004, as well as reaching the semi-finals of the Australian Open four times.

The American also has one of the most impressive Davis Cup records among the top 10 players. Only John McEnroe and Andre Agassi have clinched more rubbers for the United States than Roddick, who spearheaded the nation to their first Davis Cup victory in 12 years in 2007, ending the longest spell in the history of the competition in which the founding nation has gone without the title.

Roddick is regarded as one of the most attacking players in the game. "My aggression out there is my weapon," he once said. "I think it's more letting them know that I'm not going to let them get away with something, and I'm not just going to kind of poke it back and be content to stay in rallies."

Early in his career he was widely criticised for being too reliant on his serve and forehand to win matches. But, with the help of a string of high-profile coaches including tennis gurus Brad Gilbert and Larry Stefanki and American tennis great Jimmy Connors, his game has improved year on year.

Roddick proved himself to be a complete tennis player in the 2009 Wimbledon final when he pushed Federer to five sets for the first time in his career with a superb all-court display, eventually losing 16-14 in the final set.

Roddick is one of the most celebrated American athletes in any sport, having graced the pages of non-sporting magazines such as *Vogue* and *Rolling Stone*. He has put his fame to good use – his charity The Andy Roddick Foundation has raised over US$10 million for children's charitable causes since 2001.

Both on and off court, Roddick is famed for his quick wit and sense of humour and has even hosted the hit US comedy sketch show *Saturday Night Live*. In one outburst at a line judge, he offered children the world over some sage advice: "Stay in school kids, or you'll end up being an umpire!" ●

> 66 **My aggression out there is my weapon, I'm not just going to poke it back and be content to stay in rallies** 99

Dinara holds the 2009 Rogers Cup trophy

DINARA SAFINA

DID YOU KNOW?

Dinara and her brother Marat played together in the Hopman Cup and are the first brother and sister in the history of the modern game to hold world No.1 rankings.

RECORD BREAKER ★

Safina was the first player in tour history to defeat three world No.1s in the same season 2008 – Justine Henin, Maria Sharapova and Jelena Jankovic

PROFILE

Dinara Safina

27 April 1986

Moscow, Russia

5' 11 ½" (182cm)

154.5lbs (70kg)

Right-handed, two-handed backhand

2000

www.dsafina.com

Born into a tennis playing family, Russian Dinara Safina has reached the top of the women's game

When Dinara Safina claimed the World No.1 ranking in April 2009 she made history. Not only had she beaten three different reigning World No.1s to get to the top but with her brother Marat Safin, who had been World No.1 in the men's rankings in 2000, the pair became the only brother and sister in tennis history to occupy the World No.1 ranking.

Safina's father and mother both played tennis. Her father is now director of a tennis club in Moscow and her mother is a tennis coach. Dinara and her elder brother Marat, six years her senior, were introduced to tennis at a young age. Dinara played her first events on the ITF circuit in 2000 and was runner up at Junior Wimbledon as a 15 year old. By 2001, she had played her first tour qualifying events in Madrid and Moscow and she claimed her first singles title on the clay in Sopot, Poland the following year. That was the same year that she finished in the Top 100 for the first time.

Dinara crept up the world rankings for the next three years cracking the Top 20

Dinara enjoying time off court

On the clay at Roland Garros where Safina has contested two Grand Slam finals

HISTORY BOOK

- CAREER SINGLES TITLES: 12
- GRAND SLAM SINGLES TITLES: 0

- GRAND SLAM SINGLES RECORD

Australian Open:	Final 2009
Roland Garros:	Final 2009, Final 2008
Wimbledon:	Third Round 2008
US Open:	Semi-Final 2008

> ❝ She has showed a consistency in her results and she is one of the most industrious players on the women's tour ❞

in 2005. In 2007 she won a Grand Slam doubles titles with Frenchwoman Natalie Dechy at the US Open. But it was as a 22 year old in 2008 that she really hit the headlines. She finished the year ranked three. She won four WTA titles and became the winner of the US Open Series. She beat Frenchwoman Marion Bartoli into second place in the event that links 10 hard court tournaments with the US Open, by winning at Los Angeles and Montreal.

2008 was a great year for Dinara for several other reasons. Not only did she make it to the final at Roland Garros and the semi-final at the US Open, she was part of a trio of Russian women tennis medallists at the Beijing Olympics. Elena Dementieva took gold, Dinara the silver and Vera Zvonareva the bronze. The Russian team was victorious in the Fed Cup and although Safina did not play in the final match she was part of the squad that won.

Safina also qualified for the 2008 season-ending championships that were held in Doha for the first time.

By April 2009 Dinara was at the top of the world rankings. She may not have yet won a Grand Slam title, but she showed a consistency in her results and she is one of the most industrious players on the women's tour.

Off court Safina is close to the other Russian women players, counting Elena Vesnina and Svetlana Kuznetsova as friends. She also likes to play soccer, but she keeps most of her life private. One thing is for sure – she is delighted to have reached the top of the women's game and come out of her brother's shadow. A colourful character, Marat retired from the Tour in 2009. The brother and sister team did play together in the Hopman Cup at the start of that year.

According to Dinara having an older brother was good and bad: "it helped you at first, but then I wanted to be better, so I put more pressure on myself to be better," she remarked. "It made me want to be recognised as my own person, and now I'm there." Nobody can argue with that. ●

The message I like to convey to women and girls across the globe is that there is no glass ceiling

VENUS WILLIAMS

PROFILE

Venus Ebony Starr Williams
17 June 1980
Lynwood, California, USA
6' 1" (185cm)
160lbs (72.5kg)
Right-handed, two-handed backhand
1994
www.venuswilliams.com

Venus with the Wimbledon Trophy, which she has won five times

DID YOU KNOW?
Venus Williams turned pro at 14 years of age and beat a player ranked in the world's top 50 in her first match.

Venus at the US Open

HISTORY BOOK

- **CAREER SINGLES TITLES: 41**
- **GRAND SLAM SINGLES TITLES: 7**
- **GRAND SLAM SINGLES RECORD**

Australian Open:	Final 2003
Roland Garros:	Final 2002
Wimbledon:	2000, 2001, 2005, 2007, 2008
US Open:	2000, 2001

With more WTA singles titles than any other active player on the women's tour, the older of the two Williams sisters is a legend in the making

She talks about the Wimbledon trophy she won in 2005 as the prize that helped make her as a person: "It was a really outrageous way to win. I keep that trophy by my bed. That's the only one I keep that close to me." Venus Williams may have won five Wimbledon titles but coming back from match point down to beat Lindsay Davenport in the final that year is a reminder of the incredible staying power of the American.

Born in 1980, a year older than sister and tennis rival Serena, Venus arrived on the scene in 1994 as a 14 year old when she notched up her first professional match victory in Oakland, California. It was three years later at the US Open in 1997 when she began to break records. She was the first unseeded finalist in the Open era. She finished the year just outside the world's Top 20. From there she never looked back and by August 2009 Williams had 41 WTA singles titles to her name, including seven Grand Slams.

Williams is not a conventional player in terms of her playing activity. She has a unique approach. "If I want to play, I play. If I don't, I won't. If I want to go to school, if I want to retire, I'll do what's important to me, not what is conventional," she said.

While amassing her records, in December 2007 she received her associate degree in fashion design from the Art Institute of Fort Lauderdale and she also launched her EleVen clothing line. She also started V Starr Interiors, an interior design company in Florida, specialising in residential design.

On court her athletic ability is awesome. Venus currently holds the record for the fastest-ever serve on tour at 130mph (209kph). Her playing style is aggressive, mixing power and agility with an ability to go to the net and volley as well as attacking from the baseline. At 6' 1" she has a great reach which makes her intimidating at the net for her opponents.

Williams has yet to win the women's singles titles at the Australian Open or Roland Garros. She won the mixed doubles events at both of those tournaments in 1998. A regular partner with sister Serena in the doubles, Venus has won 15 doubles titles. In 1998 they won their first doubles title in Oklahoma City, USA and Zurich, Switzerland. They won Olympic gold together in 2000 and 2008. Venus also won Olympic gold for the women's singles in 2000.

It is Wimbledon where Venus has had most of her success and it is her favourite tournament. When she won her fourth Wimbledon title in 2007 she was on her way back from injury. Nobody expected her to win but in a stunning run of matches and a final against the French-woman Marion Bartoli, which she won 6-4 6-1, she became the lowest women's seed (23) ever to win Wimbledon.

She had to beat Serena to win the 2008 Wimbledon title and their rivalry is fascinating. They have played 21 times; Serena leads the head to head 11-10. At Wimbledon 2009 Venus defeated then world No.1 Dinara Safina in the semi-finals 6-1 6-0, which was the biggest win ever over a reigning world No.1. Lasting just 53 minutes, it was the shortest semi-final match recorded at Wimbledon. However, Venus lost the final to Serena.

Venus Williams has made a huge mark on women's tennis. Off court she campaigned hard for equal prize money and lobbied hard to get equal prize money for women at Wimbledon and Roland Garros. It was introduced in 2007 and it was fitting that it was Venus who won the Wimbledon title that year. Deserved for a player who sees herself as a role model. In her words: "The message I like to convey to women and girls across the globe is that there is no glass ceiling." ●

Venus and Serena Williams in doubles action

Serena serves
at Wimbledon

DID YOU KNOW?

Serena is the only player to have won three Grand Slam titles after saving match points. 2003 Australian Open v Kim Clijsters; 2005 Australian Open v Maria Sharapova; 2009 Wimbledon v Elena Dementieva.

SERENA WILLIAMS

The "Serena Slam" has gone down in the record books as one of the achievements of a gifted player

Serena Williams was born 15 months after her tennis playing sister Venus and was the youngest of five sisters. She has amassed 34 WTA singles titles, 11 of which are Grand Slam titles. She has already taken her place in tennis history and is still active on the Tour.

Coached, like Venus, by her father Richard Williams, Serena won her first Grand Slam title aged 17 when she triumphed at the 1999 US Open on only her second visit to Flushing Meadows. She beat Martina Hingis in the final 6-1 4-6 6-3. She waited three years for her next Grand Slam title when in 2002 she won the French Open.

2002 was a very special year for Serena. She won three of the four Grand Slam titles and went on to complete the list by winning the Australian Open in 2003. Technically this was not a Calendar Grand Slam, as injury kept her out of the

PROFILE

Serena Jamika Williams
26 September 1981
Saginaw, Miami, Florida, USA
5' 9" (175cm)
150lbs (68kg)
Right-handed, two-handed backhand
1995
www.serenawiliams.com

2002 Australian Open at the start of the year, but it was four consecutive major titles. Her achievement has been dubbed the "Serena Slam".

The "Serena Slam" is remarkable as each time she won one of the four titles she beat sister Venus in the final.

One of the reasons that Serena is such a successful player is her ability to come from behind to win. In the 2005 Australian Open she played Maria Sharapova in the semi-final. The Russian had beaten her in the Wimbledon final the year before and had three match points with serve at 5-4 in the third set. Serena managed to win the match 2-6 7-5 8-6.

If that was not a feat in itself, Serena then went on to beat the world No.1 Lindsay Davenport in the final despite

Ecstasy as an emotional Serena celebrates yet another title triumph

2009 Australian Open champion

> ❝ With one of the most remarkable tennis careers of all time, Serena is also one of the great characters on the tour ❞

being 2-6 2-2 and facing six break points in the fifth game. Serena won the last nine games to take the title 2-6 6-3 6-0.

Following her famous victory in 2005 injury kept Williams out of most tournaments for the next two years and by 2006 her world ranking had dropped to 140. But the comeback Queen won the 2007 Australian Open ranked No.81, beating a string of seeds before triumphing over Maria Sharapova in the final 6-1 6-2. She was ranked world No.1 by September 2008 and in 2009 she won the Australian Open and Wimbledon.

Serena has a powerful and consistent serve. She has a fastest serve recorded at 128mph (203kph). She has very strong groundstrokes and can dominate a rally from the baseline.

On court Serena has a unique style of dress. For the 2002 US Open she wore a black Lycra catsuit and at Wimbledon in 2009 she wore a white trench coat for her warm-up.

Her interest in fashion extends off court. She has designed a range of accessories, which includes handbags and jewellery, called the Serena Williams Signature Statement. At the launch of the range in 2009 she said: "I love to make a statement both on and off the court. Passion, drive and hard work have taken me down this and many other creative paths throughout my life."

In 2008 Serena co-founded the Serena Williams Secondary School in Kenya and has done other charitable work including making a donation to the school in South

Carolina where tennis legend Althea Gibson was born. (Gibson was the first African American to win Wimbledon, US and the French Open.)

With one of the most remarkable tennis playing careers of all time, Serena is not only a great player but also one of the great characters on the women's Tour. ●

HISTORY BOOK

- CAREER SINGLES TITLES: **34**
- GRAND SLAM SINGLES TITLES: **11**

- GRAND SLAM SINGLES RECORD

Australian Open:	2003, 2005, 2007, 2009
Roland Garros:	2002
Wimbledon:	2002, 2003, 2009
US Open:	1999, 2002, 2008

STATS AMAZING

In 2001 Serena became the first player in tennis history to win the season-ending championships on her debut.

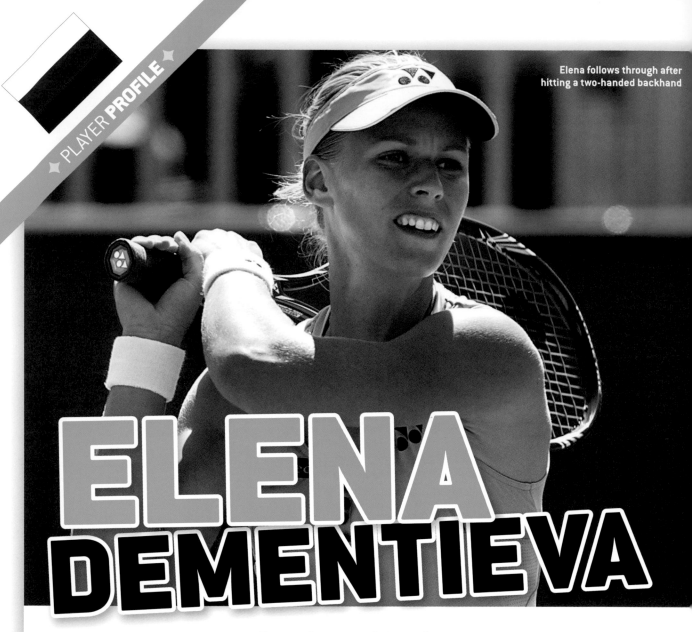

Elena follows through after hitting a two-handed backhand

ELENA DEMENTIEVA

PROFILE

Elena Vyacheslavovna Dementieva
15 October 1981
Moscow, Russia
5' 11" (180cm)
141lbs (64kg)
Right-handed, two-handed backhand
1998
www.dementieva.ru

RECORD BREAKER ★

In 2008 Dementieva appeared in her eighth year-end Championships. This is the most among active players.

One of several Russians on the Tour, she has won honours in the Fed Cup and at the Olympics and is a regular at the year-end Championships

hen she won the Olympic gold in Beijing in 2008 it was the second time Elena Dementieva had won an Olympic medal, having gained silver in 2000 in Sydney. She said: "This is for sure the biggest moment in my career, in my life. I will never forget this moment." These heartfelt words come from a player who has been on the Tour since 1999 and has had many great moments.

As a junior Elena showed her potential when she won the prestigious Orange Bowl 16s in 1996, by which time she had already played an event on the ITF Tour in Moscow. Three years later she achieved her first top 100 finish in her first year on the main Tour. She played in the main draw of all of the Slams, progressing to the third round of the US Open. She also represented Russia in the Fed Cup in a tie against the USA. Although the team was defeated 4-1, she recorded a notable victory over Venus Williams, her first win against a top 10 player.

" With a consistent game and a great record at the Olympics, Elena Dementieva is one of the best players on the women's Tour "

In 2009 Dementieva has still to add a Grand Slam title to her list of honours but she has been ranked in the top 10 since 2003, testament to the consistency of her game. One of her best years on Tour was 2004 when she reached the final at Roland Garros and the US Open. It was an historic final at Roland Garros, as it was the first time two Russians had faced one another in the final of a Slam.

Boris Yeltsin, the Russian president, came to watch Dementieva against Anastasia Myskina. Curiously, Elena also played another Russian, Svetlana Kuznetsova, in the US Open final. Dementieva had to settle for the runner-up spot on both occasions. However, as a result of her consistent results that year she was ranked No.4 in the world.

In 2005 she suffered dramatic losses at the Australian Open to Patty Schnyder

6-7(6), 7-6(4), 6-2, despite having led 7-6, 4-0, and at Roland Garros in the third round to the Kazakhstan player Elena Likhovtseva. She then lost in three sets to Myskina at Wimbledon 1-6, 7-6 (9), 7-5, failing to take two match points in the second set tie-break. Despite all of that she then played a heroic Fed Cup match against France. She won her singles matches against Mary Pierce and Amelie Mauresmo and notched up a significant doubles victory with Dinara Safina. The final score in the tie was 3-2 and the Russians won a second straight Fed Cup.

The Olympic gold medal is a highlight in Dementieva's career. In Beijing she defeated Serena Williams and compatriots Vera Zvonareva and Dinara Safina to take gold.

Playing in eight year-end championships is also a major achievement, as it is only the top eight players of the year who take part.

During her career Elena's offensive baseline play has been very consistent. With a stronger serve she is arguably better able to compete with the hard hitters on the tour such as the Williams sisters.

Her defeat by Serena Williams 6-7 (4), 7-5, 8-6 in the 2009 semi-finals at Wimbledon, where she held a match point, was avenged with a victory in the semi-finals at the Rogers Cup in Montreal. Dementieva then went on to beat fellow Russian Maria Sharapova in the final to record her 14th career title.

With a consistent game and a great record at the Olympics and the Fed Cup, Elena Dementieva is one of the best players on the women's Tour. ●

HISTORY BOOK

- CAREER SINGLES TITLES: **14**
- GRAND SLAM SINGLES TITLES: **0**
- GRAND SLAM SINGLES RECORD

Australian Open:	Semi-Final 2009
Roland Garros:	Final 2004
Wimbledon:	Semi-Final 2009, Semi-Final 2008
US Open:	Semi-Final 2008, Semi-Final 2005, Final 2004, Semi-Final 2000

Attending an event off court

Serving during a match

On the grass at Wimbledon

"Maria's journey to victory was the culmination of years of personal sacrifice and hard training"

PROFILE

Maria Yuryevna Sharapova
19 April 1987
Nyagan, Russia
6' 2" (188cm)
130lbs (59kg)
Right-handed, two-handed backhand
2001
www.mariasharapova.com

RECORD BREAKER

When she won Wimbledon in 2004 it was only the second time Maria had played there. At 17 she became the second youngest Wimbledon winner in the Open era after Martina Hingis, who was 16 when she lifted the trophy in 1997.

MARIA SHARAPOVA

One of the standout players on the Tour, Sharapova's impressive list of tennis honours also comes with a huge fanbase, sponsors and off court achievements

Off court Sharapova has walked along many red carpets

When Maria Sharapova won the Wimbledon title in 2004 many spectators knew little about this elegant 6ft 2in player. To lift the trophy she had beaten Lindsay Davenport and Serena Williams, then two of the best players on the tour. She had only played in SW19 once before, was seeded a lowly but lucky 13 and was only 17 years old.

Maria's journey to that sensational victory was the culmination of years of personal sacrifice and hard training. She was born in Russia but Maria and her father Yuri moved to the USA in 1994.

Maria first picked up a racket aged four, and at six years old while playing at a tennis clinic in Moscow she was spotted by legend Martina Navratilova. "She's got talent," Martina famously said to Maria's father.

Father and daughter left Russia for the USA to pursue that talent. Maria's mother remained at home. Maria was too young to train full time and had to wait until December 1995 to take up a scholarship at the Nick Bollettieri academy in Florida. She lived on campus and saw Yuri only at weekends. Maria was not re-united with

her mother until 1996 when the family moved to an apartment.

Maria had developed a prodigious talent and in 1996 she won the 16 and under girls event at the prestigious Eddie Herr Championships. She played her first International Tennis Federation Tour event at Sarasota in Florida in 2001 and played two main tour draws the following year as a 14 year old.

Although in 2003 Maria was ranked in the world's Top 50 for the first time and won two titles at Tokyo and Quebec she was not well known by the public in 2004, which turned into a spectacular year.

Maria finished 2004 ranked in the top five and, in addition to her first Grand Slam title at Wimbledon, she won four other tour titles including the end-of-year Tour Championships. Her victory in the year-end event was notable. Not only was it the first time she had participated but in the final she beat Serena Williams 4-6, 6-2, 6-4 having trailed 4-0 in the third set.

By 2005 Maria had achieved the world No.1 ranking – the first Russian woman to achieve such a feat – and she took three more singles titles. She won the 2006 US Open and although she struggled with injury in 2007 she remained in the world's

top five but had to withdraw from season-end events. In 2008 she won her third Grand Slam title in Australia and her 19th career title at Amelia Island but underwent surgery to her right shoulder at the end of 2008. Because of her injury, she had to remodel her serve but it proved very effective as she reached the quarter-finals at Roland Garros soon after her return to the tour in 2009.

Off court Maria set up the Maria Sharapova Foundation to help children achieve their dreams. In 2007 she became a goodwill ambassador for the United Nations Development Programme. She is a popular figure and has appeared in magazines, television shows and on red carpets all over the world. In June 2007 she was listed by *Forbes* magazine as the highest paid athlete in the world.

There is still plenty more to Sharapova's story. She is an inspiration to players and fans. As Maria commented in her mid teens: "A great tennis career is something that a 15 year old normally doesn't have. I hope my example helps other teens believe they can accomplish things they never thought possible." It also accounts for why she first shot to public attention at Wimbledon in 2004. ●

One of Maria's weapons is her double-handed backhand

HISTORY BOOK

- **CAREER SINGLES TITLES: 19**
- **GRAND SLAM SINGLES TITLES: 3**
- **GRAND SLAM SINGLES RECORD**

Australian Open:	2008
Roland Garros:	Semi-Final 2007
Wimbledon:	2004
US Open:	2006

ONES TO

MARIN CILIĆ

Date of Birth: 28 September 1988

Birthplace: Medjugorje, Bosnia & Herzegovina

Height: 6' 6" (198cm)

Weight: 180lbs (82kg)

Plays: Right-handed

Turned Pro: 2005

DID YOU KNOW?
Standing at 6' 6" Marin Cilić is one of the tallest players on the tour and has a brother called Goran.

JUAN MARTIN DEL POTRO

Date of Birth: 23 September 1998

Birthplace: Tandil, Argentina

Height: 6' 6" (198cm)

Weight: 183lbs (83kg)

Plays: Right-handed

Turned Pro: 2005

DID YOU KNOW?
The Argentine won his first Tour title in Stuttgart in July 2008 and reached his first Grand Slam final at the 2009 US Open.

LLEYTON HEWITT

Date of Birth: 24 February 1981

Birthplace: Adelaide, Australia

Height: 5' 11" (180cm)

Weight: 170lbs (77kg)

Plays: Right-handed

Turned Pro: 1998

DID YOU KNOW?
Before Lleyton pursued a tennis career aged 13, he played in Aussie Rules football. In 2005 he married actress Bec Cartwright.

GAEL MONFILS

Date of Birth: 1 September 1986

Birthplace: Paris, France

Height: 6' 4" (193cm)

Weight: 177lbs (80kg)

Plays: Right-handed

Turned Pro: 2004

DID YOU KNOW?
Gael says if he was not a tennis player he would play basketball. He's a fan of NBA team Detroit Pistons.

JO-WILFRIED TSONGA

Date of Birth: 17 April 1985

Birthplace: Le Mans, France

Height: 6' 2" (188cm)

Weight: 200lbs (91kg)

Plays: Right-handed

Turned Pro: 2004

DID YOU KNOW?
Jo-Wilfried Tsonga is nicknamed "Ali" for his resemblance to the legendary boxer Muhammad Ali.

FERNANDO VERDASCO

Date of Birth: 15 November 1983

Birthplace: Madrid, Spain

Height: 6' 2" (188cm)

Weight: 179lbs (81kg)

Plays: Left-handed

Turned Pro: 2001

DID YOU KNOW?
In 2008 Fernando helped Spain win the Davis Cup with a five set victory against Argentine Jose Acasuso.

WATCH

With so many outstanding players on the men and women's Tours there are plenty of names to watch

VICTORIA AZARENKA

31 July 1989
Minsk, Belarus
5' 10" (180cm)
132lbs (60kg)
Right-handed, two-handed backhand
2003

DID YOU KNOW?
In 2009 Azarenka won the Sony Ericsson Open in Miami, when she defeated Serena Williams 6-3, 6-1.

KIM CLIJSTERS

8 June 1983
Bilzen, Belgium
5' 8 1/2" (174cm)
150lbs (68kg)
Right-handed, two-handed backhand
1997

DID YOU KNOW?
In August 2009 Clijsters returned to the tour following retirement and the birth of her daughter and won the 2009 US Open.

ANA IVANOVIC

6 November 1987
Belgrade, Serbia
6' (184cm)
152lbs (69kg)
Right-handed, two-handed backhand
2003

DID YOU KNOW?
Ana's 2008 Grand Slam title win at Roland Garros took her to No.1 in the world rankings.

JELENA JANKOVIC

28 February 1985
Belgrade, Serbia
5' 9 1/2" (177cm)
130lbs (59kg)
Right-handed, two-handed backhand
2000

DID YOU KNOW?
At Wimbledon 2007 Jelena Jankovic won the Mixed Doubles championship with Britain's Jamie Murray.

SVETLANA KUZNETSOVA

27 June 1985
St. Petersburg, Russia
5' 8 1/2" (174cm)
161lbs (73kg)
Right handed, two-handed backhand
2000

DID YOU KNOW?
Her family are talented cyclists and her mother is a six-time world champion and holder of 20 records.

VERA ZVONAREVA

7 September 1984
Moscow, Russia
5' 7 3/4" (172cm)
130 1/2lbs (59.1 kg)
Right-handed, two-handed backhand
2000

DID YOU KNOW?
Vera Zvonareva won an Olympic bronze in the women's singles in Beijing 2008 and had her first top 10 season in 2008.

1981: Borg with the French Open trophy which he won six times in total

WHERE IS HE NOW?

Borg is involved in the Bjorn Borg Clothing Company and he has been playing on the seniors tour. He lives in Sweden with his family. He told *The Times* newspaper in 2009 "I still play tennis for exercise. I love the sport and love playing".

BJORN BORG

With many records broken before his 21st birthday and retired by the age of 25, no other player has achieved so much so quickly

Despite walking away from the sport in 1981 at the age of just 25, Bjorn Borg is rightly remembered as a tennis legend. By then, the Swedish icon had won 11 major titles — five consecutive Wimbledon titles between 1976 and 1980 and six French Open crowns. Between 1978 and 1980 he claimed three back-to-back French Open and Wimbledon titles, conquering the clay of Roland Garros and the grass of the All England Club in the space of four weeks.

It was Borg's father, a successful amateur table tennis player, who introduced him to the game. A nine-year-old Bjorn traveled with him to one tournament where among the prizes on display was a tennis racket. Borg talked later about the moment he was inspired to play the game. "When I saw it, I

PROFILE

Bjorn Rune Borg
6 June 1956
Sodertaljie, Sweden
5' 11" (180cm)
160lbs (72kg)
Right-handed, two-handed backhand
1970
1982

wanted him to win so bad, because if he could win, I would have the racket".

Borg virtually exploded onto the tennis circuit when, as a 15 year old, he posted a victory on his Davis Cup debut for Sweden in 1972. A year later he reached the quarter-finals at Wimbledon and in 1974, shortly after turning 18, Borg claimed his first Grand Slam title at the French Open.

In his early days Borg's style was fairly unorthodox — he started out with a double-handed forehand and backhand. But his game evolved over time, largely as a result of hard work. Borg's dedication to training and practice made him one of the fittest players on tour, as well as one of the most consistent: prior

Borg's athletic movement and anticipation around the court are legendary

DID YOU KNOW?

When Borg won Wimbledon in 1976 he did not drop a set in the whole tournament.

HISTORY BOOK

- CAREER SINGLES WIN-LOSS: **606-123**
- CAREER SINGLES TITLES: **62**

- GRAND SLAM TITLES: **11**

Australian Open:	Third Round 1974
Roland Garros:	1974, 1975, 1978, 1979, 1980, 1981
Wimbledon:	1976, 1977, 1978, 1979, 1980
US Open:	Final 1976, Final 1978, Final 1980, Final 1981

❝ **I was this young Swedish guy with long hair and suddenly it went mad and there were girls everywhere** ❞

to his 1976 Wimbledon victory, he famously practised his serve for two hours a day for two weeks.

In the space of his 12-year career he left a lasting mark on the game, and not just for his tennis ability. He was tall and striking with shoulder-length blond hair and piercing blue eyes, and became a 1970s icon as he attracted a whole new audience to the sport. When he arrived at Wimbledon as a 17 year old he was mobbed like a rock star. As he recalls, "I was this young Swedish guy with long hair, and suddenly it went mad and there were girls everywhere." Tennis had never seen anything like this – certainly not on the lawns of the All England Club!

On court, his unwavering composure and calm, unemotional and restrained manner earned him the nickname "the Ice Man", in stark contrast to that of some of his opponents – most notably John McEnroe, Jimmy Connors and Ilie Nastase. This, combined with his competitive edge, speed around the court and consistent strokes quickly helped him become a great player.

Borg's rivalry with John McEnroe was his most intense, and their 1980 Wimbledon final is still regarded by many as the best Wimbledon final ever. The 34-point fourth set tie-break, won by McEnroe after saving five championship points, is one of the most memorable moments in tennis history.

A year later, the American ended Borg's five-year 41-match winning streak at Wimbledon in the final to take the title. A few months later, McEnroe subjected the Swede to his fourth US Open final defeat. With that, aged just 25 and still ranked No.1 in the world, Borg shocked the world and effectively turned his back on the game. After playing just one tournament in 1982 Borg announced his retirement in January 1983, leaving behind a string of incredible records. ●

STATS AMAZING

Borg holds a Davis Cup record for most consecutive singles wins with 33.

WHERE IS HE NOW?

Lives in Los Angeles with his actress wife Bridgette Wilson and their two children. In recent years has played occasional exhibition matches against the likes of Federer, Safin and Agassi.

Sampras had one of the best serves the game has ever seen

PETE SAMPRAS

The 14-time Grand Slam champion ended his career in fairytale fashion in New York where it had all started – with victory over rival and friend Andre Agassi

During the course of his 15-year career, Pete Sampras rewrote the record books of men's tennis. His 14 Grand Slam titles and 286 weeks as world No.1 are testament to his dominance of the men's game during the 1990s, but fail to complete the story of this born winner.

Sampras' precocious talent blossomed following his Greek-American family's relocation from Washington DC to the sunny climes of California when he was seven years old. It was here that Peter Fischer honed the young American's talent, later converting Sampras' two-handed backhand to one-handed with the express intention of improving his pupil's Wimbledon prospects. In 1988 he turned professional and two years later beat Andre Agassi in the US Open final, becoming the youngest men's champion in the history of the event.

Surprisingly, Sampras recalls a defeat as the most significant match of his career – the 1992 US Open final, where the American lost to defending champion Stefan Edberg. "I just didn't dig deep enough," he remembers. It was a timely wake-up call for the 21 year old – second best was no longer good enough. "If that loss hadn't happened, I wouldn't have achieved what I achieved." From then on, Sampras devoted himself to becoming the greatest tennis player in history.

A year later, the Sampras era began with his first victory at Wimbledon. By the turn of the millennium, the name Sampras had become synonymous with the Championships; between 1993 and 2000, he lifted the Challenge Trophy seven times. Only once did he fail to reach the final in those eight years, beaten by eventual champion Richard Krajicek in the 1996 quarter-finals.

Sampras also claimed five US Open crowns and two Australian Open titles, but never conquered the clay courts of Roland Garros to complete his career Grand Slam. Despite an ill-suited game for the surface, Sampras claimed his two singles and the doubles rubber during the 1995 Davis Cup final victory over Russia on clay.

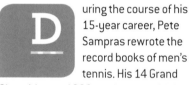

PROFILE

Peter Sampras
12 August 1971
Washington, USA
6' 1" (185cm)
170lbs (77kg)
Right-handed, one-handed backhand
1988
2002
www.petesampras.com

RECORD BREAKER ⭐

Sampras is the youngest ever US Open champion, winning in 1990 aged 19 years and 28 days. With his 2002 US Open title, "Pistol Pete" became only the second player to have won a Grand Slam in his teens, twenties and thirties.

"You kind of live and die by the serve," he once said, and it was an approach that served the American well. Sampras made his serve virtually unreadable by training himself to decide where he planned to hit the ball only when it was in the air. But it was his second serve – almost as powerful and accurate as the first – that was considered one of his deadliest weapons, backed up with a complete repertoire of volleys and a trademark slam-dunk smash that made him arguably the greatest serve-volleyer of all time.

Sampras was notorious for producing his best tennis on the most crucial points and in the biggest matches, which goes some way to explaining his formidable career statistics. He had an uncanny ability to hit aces at critical moments, on both first and second serves, and his running forehand drive could turn a defensive position on its head in an instant. "The difference of great players is at a certain point in a match they raise their level of play and maintain it," he said. "Lesser players play great for a set."

Despite being famed for his Wimbledon exploits, perhaps Sampras' finest moment came in his final act. Having not won a single title since Wimbledon in 2000, he entered the 2002 US Open as an outsider, ranked No.17 in the world and sliding. But he capped an incredible run to the final with victory against great rival, compatriot and friend Andre Agassi – the man he had beaten for his first title 12 years earlier. It was to be Sampras' final competitive match.

Despite being not just one of the greatest tennis players of all time but one of the finest athletes of his era, Sampras largely shunned the spotlight. "I let my racket do the talking," was his take on fame. "That's what I am all about, really – I just go out and win tennis matches." ●

66 Two years after turning professional Sampras became the youngest men's champion in US Open history

Sampras celebrates victory at the US Open, which he won five times

HISTORY BOOK

- CAREER SINGLES WIN-LOSS: **762-222**
- CAREER SINGLES TITLES: **64**

- GRAND SLAM TITLES: **14**

Australian Open:	1997, 1994
Roland Garros:	Semi-Final 1996
Wimbledon:	2000, 1999, 1998, 1997, 1995, 1994, 1993
US Open:	2002, 1996, 1995, 1993, 1990

Celebrating one of 60
career singles titles

**WHERE IS
HE NOW?**
Lives in Las Vegas with wife
Steffi Graf and their two children.
Famed for his youth charity
work, he opened a
high school for at-risk
children in 2001.

ANDRE AGASSI

The young rebel became one of the sport's great statesmen after choosing substance over style

The last of America's golden generation of players and one of the most exciting entertainers in the game, Andre Agassi transformed himself from a style-conscious tennis punk to a world-beating role model during the course of his rollercoaster 21-year career.

Agassi's great strength was his ability to strike the ball early. Unlike traditional counterpunchers, Agassi stood close to the baseline, which allowed him to hit angled drives and outmanoeuvre more powerful opponents, denying them the time to recover their position. His razor-sharp reflexes, compact swing style and incredible strength also made him one of the game's greatest returners.

The style was the result of hours spent hitting machine-fed drives under the watchful eye of his father Mike – a former Iranian Olympic wrestler – who drilled his son relentlessly. "We played before school, we played after school," Agassi remembers. "We woke up. We played tennis. We brushed our teeth – in that order."

Perhaps as a reaction to his regimented upbringing, Agassi displayed a rebellious streak when he broke into the professional

 **Razor-sharp reflexes, a compact swing and incredible strength made him one of the game's greatest returners**

PROFILE

Andre Kirk Agassi
29 April 1970
Las Vegas, Nevada, USA
5' 11" (181cm)
180lbs (80kg)
Right-handed, two-handed backhand
1986
2006

ranks as a 16 year old in 1986. He became as notorious for his long bottle-blond hair and zany outfits – famously wearing neon pink cycling shorts underneath a pair of denim shorts on court – as for his meteoric rise up the rankings.

Despite a string of Grand Slam semi-final and final appearances, questions about his brash attitude remained. He fronted a global advertising campaign with the slogan 'Image is Everything', and refused to play at Wimbledon between 1988 and 1990 in protest at the all-white dress

With a unique sense of style, Agassi's 1980's image is iconic

Having a laugh with wife Steffi Graf

HISTORY BOOK

- CAREER SINGLES WIN-LOSS: 870-274
- CAREER SINGLES TITLES: 60

- GRAND SLAM TITLES: 8

Australian Open:	2003, 2001, 2000, 1995
Roland Garros:	1999
Wimbledon:	1992
US Open:	1999, 1994

code. Ironically, given his relationship with the event and supposedly unsuited baseliner style of play, he won his first Grand Slam at Wimbledon in 1992.

Agassi's decision to start working with coach Brad Gilbert – a former world No.4 who had a reputation for maximising his limited talent – proved to be a masterstroke. He won his first US Open in 1994, and claimed his third Grand Slam crown on his first appearance at the Australian Open in 1995. A year later, Agassi won the gold medal at the Atlanta Olympics to cap an incredible four years.

Agassi's cross-culture appeal and fierce on-court rivalry with Pete Sampras is credited with boosting the popularity of tennis during the 1990s, but with his newfound fame came a new set of challenges. Agassi became a gossip-column celebrity and his marriage to model-actress Brooke Shields in 1997 coincided with a staggering career slump. Having been world No.1 in 1995, Agassi spiralled to No.141 in the rankings by the end of a trophy-less 1997. Many considered his career to be finished.

But in 1998 Agassi dedicated himself to tennis again, returning fitter, mentally tougher and stronger than ever before. "I had to put in the time to get back – and it was a grind," he recalls. "It meant training and sweating every day. But I was completely committed to working out to prove to myself that I still could do it." Agassi and Shields divorced in 1999 and he began dating Steffi Graf, marrying her in 2001.

Sampras may have dominated the 1990s, but with victory at the 1999 French Open Agassi become only the fifth man to complete his career Grand Slam – a feat Sampras never achieved. He then reached the next three Grand Slam finals, beaten at Wimbledon by Sampras before winning in New York and Melbourne.

Agassi didn't enter the Australian Open for the first eight years of his career, but emerged as the event's greatest modern champion. From 2000, the American went undefeated for a record 21 matches, winning his eighth and last Grand Slam title there in 2003. Later that year, aged 33 years and 13 days, he became the oldest ever world No.1.

Injuries caught up with Agassi and his ranking began to slide, but he managed to mount one last challenge at the 2005 US Open, where he lost the final to Roger Federer. Hampered by a chronic back injury, he retired a year later following a second-round defeat in New York, after which he received an eight-minute standing ovation from the crowd – a fitting tribute for one of the great ambassadors of the game. ●

RECORD BREAKER ★

Andre Agassi is the only man to have completed the Golden Slam – winning all four majors and the Olympic tennis gold medal during his career.

Rod Laver with Britain's 1977 Wimbledon
champion, Virginia Wade, at the 40th
anniversary celebrations of the US Open

**WHERE IS
HE NOW?**

Resides in Carlsbad, California.
In 2000, Melbourne Park
renamed Center Court the Rod
Laver Arena, and adidas still
sell his signature tennis
shoes as part of their
retro range.

The Australian's
1969 Grand Slam was
the crowning glory of a
remarkable career
that spanned the dawn
of the Open era

ROD LAVER

o debate about the greatest tennis player of all time is complete without mentioning the name Rod Laver. The Australian is the last player to complete a Grand Slam of the majors in a single season, and the only player to achieve the feat twice – in 1962 and 1969.

His 11 Slams put him joint-fourth on the all-time list of men's Grand Slam champions, level with Bjorn Borg and behind Roy Emerson, Pete Sampras and Roger Federer. But those achievements are all the more remarkable given that from 1963 to 1967 Laver was exiled from competing at the Grand Slams for joining the professional ranks.

At only 5ft 8in tall Laver was diminutive by today's standards, but the left-hander was a tenacious competitor and incredibly fit. His left forearm was so well developed that it looked visibly different to his right, and his powerful wrist allowed him to hit the ball with topspin on both his forehand and backhand – a relatively new technique at that time.

Like many players of his era, Laver was a serve-volleyer. At that time, three of the four Slams were played on grass – with Roland Garros the clay-court exception

PROFILE

Rodney George Laver
9 August 1938
Queensland, Australia
5' 8" (172cm)
Left-handed, one handed-backhand
1962
1979

– but the playing lawns were far more difficult to maintain in those days. "The grass was a tricky surface, but I was comfortable on it," remembers Laver. "You learned to serve and volley – you didn't want to let the ball bounce. I mean, today Wimbledon's grass looks like a billiard table!"

Laver, nicknamed "Rocket" by fellow Australian and coaching legend Harry Hopman, mastered much more than just volleys. He had the complete repertoire of shots when he joined the international tennis circuit in 1956, including a superb running backhand. In his early career he sometimes paid the price for attempting the spectacular rather than playing the percentages, but when he began taking a tactical approach to his tennis, the combination was devastatingly effective.

The Australian played during the rise of professional tennis. Professional tennis

Rod Laver holds the Wimbledon trophy aloft

"There is no way of knowing what Laver might have achieved had he been eligible to compete at more of the majors"

players were excluded from amateur tournaments, including the Slams, until the Open era began in 1968. By 1962 many of the top players – including Laver's compatriots Ken Rosewall and Lew Hoad – had turned professional, leaving Laver, who by now had two Slams to his name, as the best amateur player in the world. He won 22 of his 54 amateur titles that year alone, including all four Slams for his first Grand Slam. At the end of the season, aged 24 and with an incredible 176-15 win-loss record, Laver decided to turn professional.

Back among the greatest players of his generation, Laver found a fresh challenge. Rosewall and Hoad had the measure of him in 1963, but by 1965 Laver was crowned world No.1. By the end of 1967, he had 69 professional titles, including the so-called 'professional Grand Slam' after winning the Wembley Championships, US

Professional Championships and French Professional Championships.

The dawn of the Open era allowed Laver to return to the Slams, and the Australian became the first Open-era Wimbledon champion, beating the world's No.1 amateur Arthur Ashe in the final. A year later, Laver completed a second Grand Slam, this time contested by amateurs and professionals.

After claiming the Australian and French Open titles and defending his Wimbledon crown, Laver faced Roche in the final of the US Open to complete the quartet. After two days of heavy rain and under a grey sky, Laver put on spiked trainers after losing the first set 9-7 to help him deal with the sodden court. He went on to win the last three sets 6-1, 6-3, 6-2. There was little celebration of his achievements at the time, but his fellow competitors recognised just what the 30 year old had accomplished.

HISTORY BOOK

- CAREER SINGLES WIN-LOSS: **392-99**
- CAREER SINGLES TITLES: **40**
  [ATP-SANCTIONED EVENTS IN THE OPEN ERA]

- GRAND SLAM TITLES: **5**

Australian Open:	1969
Roland Garros:	1969
Wimbledon:	1969, 1968
US Open:	1969

There is no way of knowing what Rod Laver might have achieved had he been eligible to compete in the 20 Slams between 1963 and 1967. That no other man has repeated the Grand Slam since 1969 shows just how rare and special a player Laver was – the standout talent of his generation, and an inspirational figure within the world of tennis. ●

RECORD BREAKER

Rod Laver was the first tennis player to earn US$1,000,000 in prize money. During his career he accumulated US$1,564,213 in winnings – less than the prize money awarded to the US Open champion today.

2008 US Open: King acknowledges the crowd at the 40th anniversary celebration of Open tennis

BILLIE JEAN KING

WHERE IS SHE NOW?
Billie Jean King lives in the USA and is still very involved with tennis. In 2008 she published her eighth book entitled *Pressure is a Privilege*.

Ranked in the top 10 for 17 years as a player, this amazing American was also responsible for modernising the game

Billie Jean King was not only a great tennis player but off court she was, and still is, a campaigner for social change and equality. She won 12 Grand Slam singles titles and is possibly best known for her tennis match against a

PROFILE

Billie Jean King
22 November 1943
Long Beach, California, USA
5' 4" (164cm)
134lbs (60.7kg)
Right-handed, one-handed backhand
1968
1983

man, Bobby Riggs in 1973, and for starting the women's professional Tour.

King played in her first Grand Slam in 1959 and went on in the Open era (post 1968) to amass 39 Grand Slam titles in singles, doubles and mixed doubles. She hit the ball hard and was aggressive in her play, rushing the net and gaining respect for her dislike of losing. She once famously said: "Victory is fleeting. Losing is forever." In 1971 she became the first woman in the history of sport to earn over US$100 000 in a single season.

In September 1970 she was one of nine players who broke away from the tennis establishment and accepted US$1

contracts from promoter Gladys Heldman in Houston. The revolt led to the birth of women's professional tennis with the formation of the Virginia Slims Tour and the creation of the Women's Tennis Association, which King spearheaded in 1973.

King, who received US$15,000 less than Ilie Nastase did for winning the US Open in 1972, said if the prize money wasn't equal by the next year, she wouldn't play, and she didn't think the other women would either. In 1973, the US Open became the first major tournament to offer equal prize money for men and women.

That year was a remarkable one for King. Not only did she win the singles

❝ In the '70s we had to make it acceptable for people to accept women as athletes ❞

HISTORY BOOK

- **CAREER SINGLES WIN-LOSS: 695-155**
- **CAREER SINGLES TITLES: 67**

- **GRAND SLAM TITLES: 12**

Australian Open:	1968
Roland Garros:	1968, 1972
Wimbledon:	1966, 1967, 1968, 1972, 1973, 1975
US Open:	1971, 1972, 1974

doubles and mixed doubles at Wimbledon, one of only three players to accomplish a Grand Slam triple crown in the Open era, but she also played her famous match against 55-year-old Riggs.

Riggs was a former Wimbledon champion and claimed that the women's game was inferior. On September 20th King and Riggs took to the court at the Houston Astrodome in the USA to play a match that was dubbed "Battle of the Sexes". It was watched live by 30,492 people. King defeated Riggs 6-4, 6-3, 6-3 and proved it was possible for a woman to beat a man.

While she was busy campaigning off court, her tennis playing record is one of the most successful in the Open era of tennis. In total she holds 129 singles titles which includes 12 Grand Slams. She dominated the women's game in the early 1970s until her retirement in 1983.

Even after retirement she continued to be involved with tennis. She captained the USA Fed Cup team in 1995-6 and 1998-2001 and she was the US Olympic Women's team captain in 1996 and 2000.

Her awards and achievements are too numerous to list here but perhaps the most significant was when King was awarded the Presidential Medal of Freedom, the highest civilian honour of the United States, by President Obama at the White House on August 12, 2009.

Billie Jean King made an unrivalled contribution to the development of women's tennis as well as being a great player herself. She remains an inspiration to the players on today's Tour and to many people all over the world. She is a tennis legend. ●

DID YOU KNOW?

Billie Jean King enjoyed her greatest success at Wimbledon where she holds 20 titles combined in singles, doubles and mixed doubles.

Navratilova still receives a warm welcome when she attends tennis events

WHERE IS SHE NOW?

Martina still has a high profile around tennis and is a strong advocate of health and well-being for everyone. She has written a book, *Shape Yourself*.

MARTINA
NAVRATILOVA

RECORD BREAKER ★

Navratilova holds 167 singles titles, which is more than any man or woman player.

PROFILE

Martina Navratilova

18 October 1956

Czechoslovakia (US Citizen 1981)

5' 8" (173cm)

145lbs (65kg)

Left-handed

1975

2006

www.martinanavratilova.com

No other tennis player has a career that glitters quite as much as that of Martina Navratilova

With a tennis-playing career that spans an extraordinary 33 years, Martina Navratilova is the most prolific winner of the Open era. She holds 167 singles titles, which is more than any man or woman player. She also holds 177 doubles titles, including 10 mixed doubles titles — that's a record-breaking 344 championships in total.

Navratilova was born in 1956 in Prague in the Czech Republic and she emigrated to the USA in 1975 to escape the communist system that existed in her home country.

She became an American citizen in 1981 and although she returned home triumphant to Czechoslovakia in 1986, her success was not reported there for many years while she was playing. This backdrop makes her career all the more remarkable.

Martina first attracted attention as a 16 year old when she played at the French Open in 1973 reaching the quarter-finals unseeded. That was the same year that she began her legendary rivalry with Chris Evert. By the end of the 1970s she had already cemented her place in history having won two Wimbledon titles in 1978 and 1979.

Navratilova and Chris Evert, with whom she enjoyed a 16-year rivalry on court, but the pair were great friends off it

HISTORY BOOK

- CAREER SINGLES WIN-LOSS: 1442-219
- CAREER SINGLES TITLES: 167

- GRAND SLAM TITLES: 18

Australian Open:	1981, 1983, 1985
Roland Garros:	1982, 1984
Wimbledon:	1978, 1979, 1982, 1983, 1984
	1985, 1986, 1987, 1990
US Open:	1983, 1984, 1986, 1987

and 1984. On the first occasion she did not manage to win the French Open. However, 1983 was a significant year as Martina notched up an 86-1 winning percentage that has never been equalled. In 1984 she missed out on the Australian Open when she lost in the semi-finals to Helena Sukova 1-6, 6-3, 7-5 but she had some consolation by winning the doubles with Pam Shriver.

Martina won the US Open four times, although she did not win until her 11th attempt when she beat Chris Evert 6-1, 6-3. This was one of Martina's significant wins over her rival. They met 80 times and in the final head-to-head Navratilova came out on top with 43 wins to Evert's 37.

Martina's list of records is unrivalled in the modern game. To be so dominant for so long is a feat that may never be repeated in a game where physical demands are so great. She won at least one Tour event for 21 consecutive years.

Today Navratilova promotes health and well-being for all ages and has written a book titled *Shape Yourself*. She campaigns for human rights through the Rainbow Card Affinity programme and promotes animal rescue through the Pet Care Find Sanctuary. She has also worked with artist Juro Kralik on an Art Grand Slam Collection, which has been exhibited around the world.

Navratilova's achievements make her a tennis legend and possibly the greatest player of all time. ●

Navratilova attributes her success to her coach Nancy Lieberman. In 1981 Martina said: "Even though I had won two Wimbledons she sternly lectured me that I was wasting my talent, needed to work harder than ever and give tennis total commitment."

Her achievement as a singles player was testament to her great game. She loved to volley and charged the net. Some say she is the greatest female tennis player ever. She was also a phenomenal doubles player. Her partnership with Pam Shriver resulted in 21 Grand Slam wins between 1981 and 1989.

She won her final Grand Slam title in the mixed doubles at the US Open in 2006 with another left-hander Bob Bryan. The fact that she was only a few days away

from her 50th birthday gave her another record-breaking statistic of being the oldest person to win a Grand Slam title in the Open era.

Her Wimbledon record is unrivalled. She played there 23 years and reached nine consecutive finals. Her win-loss record in singles was 120-14, doubles 80-14 and 44-9 mixed. Quite simply, she played 244 matches in SW19 and lost a mere 37.

The only prize that eluded Navratilova was a calendar Grand Slam. She came within a whisker of achieving this in 1983

> 66 **Her achievement as a singles player was testament to her great game. Some say she is the greatest female player ever** 99

Evert holds aloft the 1976 US Open trophy

DID YOU KNOW?
Evert holds the Open era record for consecutive semi-finals or better with 34 from US Open 1971 to Roland Garros 1983.

WHERE IS SHE NOW?
She has three children, and lives in Boca Raton, Florida, where she opened the Evert Tennis Academy.

CHRIS EVERT

PROFILE

Christine Marie Evert
21 December 1954
Fort Lauderdale, Florida, USA
5' 6" (168cm)
125lbs (56.6kg)
Right-handed, two-handed backhand
1972
1989

Evert with Tracy Austin at Wimbledon in 1977

With 18 Grand Slam singles titles to her name Evert was one of the most popular players on Tour

Between 1971 and 1986 Chris Evert wowed tennis fans wherever she went. With her consistent strokes and her good looks she was entertaining to watch. She won 21 Slams and notched up the highest percentage winning record in women's professional tennis history.

Evert was born into a tennis family. Her father Jimmy Evert was a coach and her sister Jeanne, with whom she played Wightman Cup in 1974, was a nationally ranked player in the USA.

Evert's first significant victory came in 1970 at a small tournament in North Carolina when the 15-year-old Evert beat Margaret Court 7-6, 7-6. At the time Court held the world No.1 ranking and had just completed her singles Grand Slam. The following year aged 16 years eight months and 20 days Evert progressed to the semi-finals of the US Open. Although she lost to Billie Jean King 6-3, 6-2 Evert had made her mark on professional tennis and established herself as a crowd favourite at

a Grand Slam event that she went on to win six times between 1975 and 1982.

What made Evert such an effective player was her consistency. She was essentially a slow court baseline specialist. She hit her strokes with accuracy and precision and rarely made mistakes. She also had a determination to win that earned her the nickname of "The Ice Maiden".

Assessing her own game she said, "I realise that a lot of my fans think my game is boring and they want me to lose, or at least for somebody to give me a good fight all the time. But this is the game I played to win. Losing hurts me. I was always determined to be the best."

Effective as she was at the baseline she also possessed a good volley, a well-disguised drop shot and her game was complete enough to win her 18 Grand Slam titles; two in Australia, seven at Roland Garros, three at Wimbledon and six in Flushing Meadow. She also won three doubles Grand Slam titles – two at the French Open and one at Wimbledon.

Her double handed-backhand, a powerful drive, was copied by many players but according to her father he advised against it. "I didn't teach the two-hander to her. She started that way because she was too weak to swing the backhand with one hand. I hope she'd change – but how can I argue with this success?"

During her career Evert established two famous rivalries. The first was against the Australian player Evonne Goolagong. They first met in the 1972 Wimbledon semi-final. Goolagong won in three sets 4-6, 6-3, 6-4. They were to play one another many times and the final statistics show that of their 33 matches Evert came out on top, winning 21 of them.

The other rivalry was with Martina Navratilova. They played over 80 matches between 1973 and 1988. Evert won their first encounter and took a big early lead but Navratilova overtook her to come out ahead, 43-37, winning nine of their major final matches.

Evert's last appearance in a Grand Slam final was in Australia in 1988. She faced the 18-year-old newcomer Steffi Graf. It was a tightly fought match but Graf won 6-1, 7-6 (7-3). Evert's Grand Slam career had spanned 15 years and she finally hung up her racket in 1989.

Her record number of match wins is legendary. She won 1309 matches and lost only 146. Evert also has the best record on clay of any single surface with a 125 match-winning streak set between August 1973 and May 1979.

In 1989 Evert founded Chris Evert Charities to help children in need and in March 1996 opened the Evert Tennis Academy in Boca Raton, Florida. ●

> **66 A lot of my fans think my game is boring and want me to lose. But this is the game I played to win. Losing hurts me. 99**

HISTORY BOOK

- **CAREER SINGLES TITLES: 154**
- **GRAND SLAM SINGLES TITLES: 18**
- **GRAND SLAM SINGLES RECORD**

Australian Open:	1982, 1984
Roland Garros:	1974, 1975, 1979, 1980, 1983, 1985, 1986
Wimbledon:	1974, 1976, 1981
US Open:	1975, 1976, 1977, 1978, 1980, 1982

Graf celebrates her fifth
French Open title in 1996

**WHERE IS
SHE NOW?**

Married to Andre Agassi with
two children and lives in Las
Vegas. Played an exhibition
match at Wimbledon in
May 2009.

STEFFI GRAF

With 22 Grand Slam singles titles to her name, Steffi Graf is arguably the best female tennis player ever

Steffi Graf is one of the all time greats of modern tennis. She has a jaw-dropping 22 Grand Slam titles to her name and is the only player to have won a Golden Slam – four Slams plus an Olympic gold in the same year. The record books also show that she won each of the Slams at least four times.

Steffi Graf was introduced to tennis by her father aged three and played her first professional tournament in October 1982 aged 13. She remains the second youngest female player ever to have a ranking when at 13 years and four months she was ranked World No.124.

Her playing schedule in the early days was very limited and she didn't win any Slams until 1986. By virtue of the fact she consistently reached finals and semi-finals by 1985 her world ranking had increased to No.6.

In 1987 Graf won her first Grand Slam title defeating Martina Navratilova 6-4, 4-6, 8-6 in the French Open final. The same year she went on to win the US Open. Graf was still only 18 years old.

Steffi Graf's place in history was sealed the following year in 1988. Only six years after turning professional and at only 19 years of age, she became the only female tennis player to date to win a Golden Slam. She won all four of the major

PROFILE

Stefanie Maria Graf
14 June 1969
Bruhl, Germany
5' 9" (176cm)
132lbs (59.8kg)
Right-handed, one-handed backhand
1982
1999
www.steffi-graf.net

> 66 **Steffi was introduced to tennis by her father aged three and played her first professional tournament in 1982 aged 13** 99

In 2009 Graf and Andre Agassi teamed up to play an exhibition match under the new Centre Court roof at the All England Club

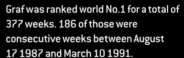

Steffi's composure on court won her many admirers

tournaments as well as an Olympic gold medal in Seoul.

Although she suffered injury during the early nineties, she had a return to form in 1993. Graf won three Grand Slams that year. She also underwent surgery on her foot as well as suffering from a back injury. She went on to win 11 Grand Slam titles in the second half of her tennis

career between 1993 and 1999. She won her final Grand Slam at Roland Garros.

Not only is Graf's individual tennis playing record exceptional but she also led Germany to victory in the 1987 and 1992 Fed Cup competition. She represented her country for seven years and her singles record was 19-2.

Announcing her retirement in August 1999, ranked World No.3, she said that she was no longer enjoying her tennis: "I have done everything I wanted to do in tennis, I feel I have nothing left to accomplish."

She had reached her ninth Wimbledon singles final where she had been defeated by Lindsay Davenport 6-4, 7-5. "After Wimbledon for the first time in my career I did not feel like going to a tournament."

Steffi Graf's tennis playing achievements are unrivalled in the modern game. Many players consider her to be the greatest female player of all

HISTORY BOOK

- CAREER SINGLES WIN-LOSS: 900-115
- CAREER SINGLES TITLES: 107

- GRAND SLAM TITLES: 22

Australian Open:	1999, 1994, 1989, 1988
Roland Garros:	1999, 1996,1995, 1993, 1988, 1987
Wimbledon:	1996, 1995, 1993, 1992, 1991, 1989, 1988
US Open:	1996, 1995, 1993, 1989, 1988

RECORD BREAKER ★

Graf was ranked world No.1 for a total of 377 weeks. 186 of those were consecutive weeks between August 17 1987 and March 10 1991.

time. She possessed a ferocious forehand (some dubbed her "Fraulein forehand"), she was quick around the court and she had a powerful and accurate serve. She worked hard at her game and her fitness.

Off court she set up a not for profit foundation Children for Tomorrow which supports children who have been traumatised by war or other crises. She now lives in Las Vegas with her husband, tennis legend Andre Agassi whom she married in 2001. She posts regular blogs on her official website about her life and the achievements of the Foundation.

Graf's dominance of the women's game in the late 1980s and 1990s remains an inspiration to many of today's players. ●

RECENT

BORIS BECKER

Date of Birth: 22 November 1967
Birthplace: Leimen, Germany
Plays: Right-handed
Turned Pro: 1984
Retired: 1999
Career Singles Titles: 49
Career Slam Titles: 6

DID YOU KNOW?

As a 17 year old Boris Becker won Wimbledon in 1985. He grew up not far from Bruhl where Steffi Graf was raised and they sometimes practised together.

JIMMY CONNORS

Date of Birth: 2 September 1952
Birthplace: Belleville, Illinois, USA
Plays: Left-handed
Turned Pro: 1972
Retired: 1992
Career Singles Titles: 107
Career Slam Titles: 8

DID YOU KNOW?

A big character on court, Connors frequently argued with officials but had a game good enough to win a record number of titles and to win the US Open five times.

STEFAN EDBERG

Date of Birth: 19 January 1966
Birthplace: Vastervik, Sweden
Plays: Right-handed
Turned Pro: 1983
Retired: 1996
Career Singles Titles: 42
Career Slam Titles: 6

DID YOU KNOW?

Although Edberg never won at Roland Garros he came close in 1989 when he lost in the final to 17-year-old Michael Chang in a five-set match.

IVAN LENDL

Date of Birth: 7 March 1960
Birthplace: Czechoslovakia (US Citizen 1992)
Plays: Right-handed
Turned Pro: 1978
Retired: 1994
Career Singles Titles: 94
Career Slam Titles: 8

DID YOU KNOW?

When he retired Lendl had a phenomenal 1279-274 singles win-loss record. The only Slam to elude him was Wimbledon, despite his reaching two finals.

JOHN MCENROE

Date of Birth: 16 February 1969
Birthplace: New York, USA
Plays: Left-handed
Turned Pro: 1978
Retired: 1992
Career Singles Titles: 77
Career Slam Titles: 7

DID YOU KNOW?

McEnroe finished in the world's top 10 for 10 years. He is now a TV tennis commentator and his brother, Patrick, seven years his junior, captained the USA Davis Cup team.

MATS WILANDER

Date of Birth: 22 August 1964
Birthplace: Vaxjo, Sweden
Plays: Right-handed
Turned Pro: 1981
Retired: 1991
Career Singles Titles: 33
Career Slam Titles: 7

DID YOU KNOW?

As an unseeded 17 year old Wilander beat Guillermo Vilas to the French Open title in 1981. In 1988 he won three Slams, but lost in the quarter-finals at Wimbledon.

GREATS

Plenty of players have made their mark. Some are still involved as players, coaches or commentators.

JENNIFER CAPRIATI

Date of Birth: 29 March 1976
Birthplace: New York, USA
Plays: Right-handed, two-handed backhand
Turned Pro: 1990
Retired: 2004
Career Singles Titles: 14
Career Slam Titles: 3

DID YOU KNOW?
Capriati reached her first Tour final aged 13 years and 11 months. After early success she left the game but returned in 2001 and won the Australian Open.

LINDSAY DAVENPORT

Date of Birth: 8 June 1976
Birthplace: Palos Verdes, USA
Plays: Right-handed, two-handed backhand
Turned Pro: 1983
Retired: 2007
Career Singles Titles: 55
Career Slam Titles: 3

DID YOU KNOW?
At 6ft 3in Davenport is one of the tallest women players. She won Olympic Gold in Atlanta in 1996. Her father Wink was a US Olympic volleyball player.

JUSTINE HENIN

Date of Birth: 1 June 1982
Birthplace: Liege, Belgium
Plays: Right-handed, one-handed backhand
Turned Pro: 1999
Retired: 2008
Career Singles Titles: 41
Career Slam Titles: 7

DID YOU KNOW?
When Henin retired in May 2008 she was ranked world No.1. After 16 months out of the game she announced her return to the 2010 Tour.

MARTINA HINGIS

Date of Birth: 30 September 1980
Birthplace: Kosice, Slovakia
Plays: Right-handed, two-handed backhand
Turned Pro: 1994
Retired: 2007
Career Singles Titles: 43
Career Slam Titles: 5

DID YOU KNOW?
Hingis won her first career Tour title aged 15 and her first Slam in Australia in 1997. Her mother, Melanie Molitor, coached her throughout her career.

ARANTXA SANCHEZ VICARIO

Date of Birth: 18 December 1971
Birthplace: Barcelona, Spain
Plays: Right-handed, two handed backhand
Turned Pro: 1985
Retired: 2002
Career Singles Titles: 29
Career Slam Titles: 4

DID YOU KNOW?
In February 1995 the Spaniard was ranked No.1 simultaneously in singles and doubles, the first Spanish player to achieve this.

MONICA SELES

Date of Birth: 2 December 1973
Birthplace: Yugoslavia (US Citizen 1995)
Plays: Left-handed, two-handed both sides
Turned Pro: 1989
Retired: 2007
Career Singles Titles: 53
Career Slam Titles: 9

DID YOU KNOW?
Had 28 months out of the game in 1993 after she was stabbed on court by a demented German spectator. She returned to win the Australian Open.

DOUBLES HEROES

Doubles is the chosen game of several inspirational players

Although the singles game is the more popular form of tennis, doubles gives players a whole new set of challenges. Players must work with a partner to beat two opponents across the net, with the outer tramlines marking the larger playing boundary.

Most players grow up playing both singles and doubles, and although many top professionals choose to specialise in one or the other, many continue to play both throughout the season. Doubles also gives men and women the chance to compete side by side, with professionals teaming up at the four Grand Slams to chase mixed doubles glory.

Described by tennis historian Bud Collins as "the people's game", doubles is a fun and social form of what is often an individual pursuit. If you are consistent, good at playing at the net and enjoy team sports, then doubles is for you!

JONAS BJORKMAN

If proof were needed that you do not need to form a long-term partnership to be a successful doubles player, Jonas Bjorkman provides it. The Swede reached No.4 in the world as a singles player, but achieved much more in doubles, winning nine major titles with four different partners. After winning back-to-back Australian Open titles with Jacco Eltingh and Pat Rafter, Bjorkman teamed up with Todd Woodbridge following Mark Woodforde's retirement, claiming a further five titles before completing his career Grand Slam at Roland Garros with Max Mirnyi.

GRAND SLAM RECORD

Career doubles titles: 54

Career Grand Slam doubles titles: 9

GRAND SLAM DOUBLES RECORD

Australian Open: 2001, 1999, 1998

Roland Garros: 2006, 2005

Wimbledon: 2004, 2003, 2002

US Open: 2003

BOB AND MIKE BRYAN

Born two minutes apart, American twin brothers Bob and Mike Bryan are famed for their all-out attacking style of play. Left-handed Bob is one inch taller than right-handed Mike, and as juniors their parents forbade them from playing against one another, taking turns to give each other walkovers (an unopposed victory). As a junior doubles team they won over 100 titles including the US Open. The Bryans completed a career Grand Slam in 2006 with victory at Wimbledon, and won the 2007 Davis Cup for US with team-mates Andy Roddick and James Blake.

GRAND SLAM RECORD

Career doubles titles: 54

Career Grand Slam doubles titles: 7

GRAND SLAM DOUBLES RECORD

Australian Open: 2009, 2007, 2006

Roland Garros: 2003

Wimbledon: 2006

US Open: 2008, 2005

LEANDER PAES AND MAHESH BHUPATHI

LEANDER PAES

Indian duo Mahesh Bhupathi and Leander Paes looked set to establish themselves as a formidable doubles partnership after reaching the finals of all four Slams in 1999, winning Roland Garros and Wimbledon in the process. But despite claiming a further Roland Garros title together, the pair went their separate ways after winning gold at the Asian Games. Since then both players have gone on to win Grand Slam doubles titles with new partners, and occasionally team up to represent their country.

GRAND SLAM RECORD
Career doubles titles: 23

Career Grand Slam doubles titles: 3

GRAND SLAM DOUBLES RECORD
Australian Open: Final 1999

Roland Garros: 2001, 1999 (Paes 2009)

Wimbledon: 1999

US Open: Final 1999 (Bhupathi 2002, Paes 2009, 2006)

MAHESH BHUPATHI

JOHN MCENROE AND PETER FLEMING

"The best doubles pair in the world is John McEnroe and anybody else," was fellow American Peter Fleming's modest assessment of his role in one of the most successful doubles partnerships of all time. In truth Fleming and McEnroe's technical, physical and psychological differences complemented each other perfectly, as the pair claimed four Wimbledon and three US Open titles in five years along with three Davis Cup titles.

GRAND SLAM RECORD
Career doubles titles: 51

Career Grand Slam doubles titles: 7

GRAND SLAM DOUBLES RECORD
Australian Open: Third Round 1983

Roland Garros: Did not play

Wimbledon: 1984, 1983, 1981, 1979 (McEnroe 1992)

US Open: 1983, 1981, 1979 (McEnroe 1989)

MARK WOODFORDE AND TODD WOODBRIDGE

Australian duo Todd Woodbridge and Mark Woodforde became the most successful doubles team in tennis history. Left-handed baseliner Woodforde and volley master Woodbridge landed eleven Slams together, including a record six Wimbledon titles, as well as Olympic gold in Atlanta and the 1999 Davis Cup. The pair completed a Golden Slam in 2000 when they won the French Open shortly before Woodforde retired from international tennis. Woodbridge went on to win another five Slams before leaving the game in 2005.

GRAND SLAM RECORD
Career doubles titles: 61

Career Grand Slam doubles titles: 11

GRAND SLAM DOUBLES RECORD
Australian Open: 1997, 1992 (Woodbridge 2001)

Roland Garros: 2000

Wimbledon: 2000, 1997, 1996, 1995, 1994, 1993 (Woodbridge 2004, 2003, 2002)

US Open: 1996, 1995 (Woodbridge 2003, Woodforde 1989)

WOMEN'S DOUBLES

Some of the best women's singles players have picked up honours as part of a doubles team, while Cara Black and Liezel Huber have become doubles specialists and risen to the top of the world rankings

SERENA AND VENUS WILLIAMS

GRAND SLAM RECORD
Career doubles titles: **17**
Career Grand Slam doubles titles: **10**

GRAND SLAM DOUBLES RECORD
Australian Open: **2009, 2003, 2001**
Roland Garros: **1999**
Wimbledon: **2009, 2008, 2002, 2000**
US Open: **2009, 1999**

The only women in tennis history to complete a career doubles Golden Slam, Venus and Serena Williams focus their doubles efforts on the Slams and Olympics, having played at just a handful of other events during their careers. Incredibly, the American sisters have won in all ten of their Grand Slam final appearances since 1999, as well as both the 2004 and 2008 doubles Olympic gold medals together. They both have two mixed doubles titles to their name as well, after sweeping the board in 1998 – Venus winning the Australian Open and Roland Garros with Justin Gimelstob, with Serena claiming the Wimbledon and the US Open titles partnering Max Mirnyi.

Venus and Serena discuss tactics, no one else will hear!

PAM SHRIVER AND MARTINA NAVRATILOVA

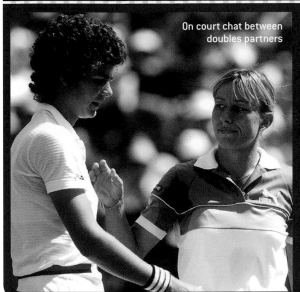

On court chat between doubles partners

Martina Navratilova and Pam Shriver are one of the most decorated doubles partnerships in tennis history, claiming seven Australian Open titles, five Wimbledon crowns, and four wins at both Roland Garros and the US Open together. American Shriver played both singles and doubles, but her low sliced drives were most effective on a doubles court, while Navratilova, granted American citizenship in 1981 after leaving communist Czechoslovakia in 1975, dominated both disciplines and was ranked world No.1 in both singles and doubles, completing a sweep of the Grand Slam singles, doubles and mixed doubles titles – the so-called "boxed set" – in 2003, winning the Australian Open mixed doubles with Leander Paes.

GRAND SLAM RECORD

Career doubles titles 79

Career Grand Slam doubles titles 20

GRAND SLAM DOUBLES RECORD

Australian Open 1989, 1988, 1987, 1985, 1984, 1983, 1982 (Navratilova 1980)

Roland Garros 1988, 1987, 1985, 1984 (Navratilova 1986, 1982, 1975)

Wimbledon 1986, 1984, 1983, 1982, 1981 (Navratilova 1979, 1976)

US Open 1987, 1986, 1984, 1983 (Shriver 1991, Navratilova 1990, 1989, 1980, 1978, 1977)

CARA BLACK AND LIEZEL HUBER

GRAND SLAM RECORD

Career doubles titles 22

Career Grand Slam doubles titles 4

GRAND SLAM DOUBLES RECORD

Australian Open 2007

Roland Garros Final 2005

Wimbledon 2007, 2005

US Open 2008

www.blackandhuber.com

Having played together occasionally since 1998, the nimble Zimbabwean Cara Black and powerful South Africa-born American Liezel Huber established themselves as a partnership in 2005. The decision was flourishing when the duo reached the Roland Garros final and then won Wimbledon, before a knee injury sidelined Huber for six months. The pair reformed in 2007 and immediately claimed the Australian Open before winning a second Wimbledon crown and being ranked as the world's No.1 doubles pair in 2008-9.

Before they became a team both players had successful tennis careers. Cara Black has won 51 doubles titles in total and also has three mixed doubles titles to her name. In 2004 she won the US Open with Leander Paes, and she won titles at Roland Garros in 2002 and Wimbledon in 2004 with her brother Wayne Black. In her career she has also had successful women's doubles partnerships with Rennae Stubbs, Elena Likhovtseva and Irina Selyutina.

Liezel Huber has 39 doubles titles to her name. She has won one mixed doubles title when she partnered Bob Bryan at Roland Garros in 2009. In June 2007 she became a US Citizen and played in the US Olympic team in 2008. She set up the Huber Tennis Ranch in March 2008.

> ❝ I like the partnership. I enjoy having someone on court out there and building on teamwork. A lot more goes on, you have these quick rallies at the net, and you get different styles. I think it's a mixture of all that that keeps it exciting ❞
>
> CARA BLACK ON WHY SHE LIKES DOUBLES

> ❝ What makes me a good doubles players is that I feel comfortable out there. I can compete with anybody, whether it's the number one singles player or doubles player. On a singles court, I wasn't that comfortable, that's why I don't mind being called a doubles specialist ❞
>
> LIEZEL ON HER SKILLS AS A DOUBLES PLAYER

2008 US Open Doubles champions

HEATHER WATSON

Australia's Bernard Tomic

Many professional players spent time on the junior circuit. For the under 18s it's a taste of future life on Tour

During the second week of the four Grand Slam events, players who are under 18 take to the courts to play in their own tournament. Just as in the main event, there is a girls and boys singles event as well as a girls and boys doubles event.

The roll of honour for these events can provide a useful insight into who may be the game's future stars. That is not to say that all world No.1s enjoyed success on the junior circuit, or that promising juniors are guaranteed to make the transition to the senior game.

One of the biggest challenges for a player making the transition from junior to senior tennis is the ability to play good players week in and week

RISING STARS

?? DID YOU KNOW?
British Girl Heather Watson was the 2009 US Open girls champion.

India's Yuki Bhambri

JUNIOR BOYS AND GIRLS ROLL OF HONOUR

AUSTRALIAN OPEN

YEAR	BOYS	GIRLS
2009	Yuki Bhambri (IND)	Ksenia Pervak (RUS)
2008	Bernard Tomic (AUS)	Arantxa Rus (NED)
2007	Brydan Klein (AUS)	Anastasia Pavlyuchenkova (RUS)
2006	Alexandre Sidorenko (FRA)	Anastasia Pavlyuchenkova (RUS)
2005	Donald Young (USA)	Victoria Azarenka (BLR)
2004	Gael Monfils (FRA)	Shahar Peer (ISR)

ROLAND GARROS

YEAR	BOYS	GIRLS
2009	Daniel Berta (SWE)	Kristina Mladenovic (FRA)
2008	Tsung-Hua Yang (TPE)	Simona Halep (ROU)
2007	Vladimir Ignatic (BLR)	Alize Cornet (FRA)
2006	Martin Klizan (SVK)	Agnieszka Radwanska (POL)
2005	Marin Cilic (CRO)	Agnes Szavay (HUN)
2004	Gael Monfils (FRA)	Sesil Karatantcheva (BUL)

WIMBLEDON

YEAR	BOYS	GIRLS
2009	Andrey Kuznetsov (RUS)	Noppawan Lertcheewakarn (THA)
2008	Grigor Dimitrov (BUL)	Laura Robson (GBR)
2007	Donald Young (USA)	Ursula Radwanska (POL)
2006	Thiemo De Bakker (NED)	Caroline Wozniacki (DEN)
2005	Donald Young (USA)	Agnieska Radwanska (POL)
2004	Gael Monfils (FRA)	Kateryna Bondarenko (UKR)

US OPEN

YEAR	BOYS	GIRLS
2009	Bernard Tomic (AUS)	Heather Watson (GBR)
2008	Grigor Dimitrov (BUL)	CoCo Vandeweghe (USA)
2007	Riardas Berankis (LTU)	Kristina Kucova (SVK)
2006	Dusan Lojda (CZR)	Anastasia Pavlyuchenkova (RUS)
2005	Ryan Sweeting (BAH)	Victoria Azarenka (BLR)
2004	Andy Murray (GBR)	Sesil Karatantcheva (BUL)

out. Many emerging players comment on the intensity of the senior circuit. Some players burst through, like Maria Sharapova who in 2002 was runner-up in the girl's singles at Wimbledon and then in 2004 won The Championships aged 17. That was an exceptional achievement – most players take longer to make the transition from junior status to grand slam contender.

Caroline Wozniacki won junior Wimbledon in 2006 before joining the women's circuit the following year and reaching the top 10 in 2009. One of her observations about the transition was that when it comes to playing points and matches, "Senior players take the first opportunity they have, not the second or the third: if they have one chance they take it."

Agnieszka Radwanska echoes that sentiment. "The juniors was like a warm-up before women's tennis. Here (main Tour) it is like a job, travelling a lot, talking to the press, there is not time for everything." Now the Polish No.1, Radwanska won the 2005 junior Wimbledon and 2006 French Open girls' titles before storming up the rankings on the women's Tour.

Swedish tennis legend Stefan Edberg completed a junior Grand Slam in 1983 when he won all four boys singles titles.

GRIGOR DIMITROV

CAROLINE WOZNIACKI

LAURA ROBSON

Britain's Laura Robson has been successful as a junior and possesses a game that has caused much interest in the tennis world.

Laura Robson was born in January 1994. Although she was born in Australia she moved to Britain at a very young age and began playing tennis when she was six years old. Laura, who plays left-handed, joined the ITF Junior tour in 2007 and in 2008 won the Junior Girls Championship at Wimbledon aged 14 when she beat Noppawan Lertcheewakarn 6-3, 3-6, 6-1.

The following January Robson reached the final of the 2009 Australian Open Girls singles. She had to settle for the runner-up trophy on that occasion when the Russian Ksenia Pervak defeated her. However, given the age difference — Laura was still only 15 and Pervak was 18 — the result was not unsurprising.

Robson played her first senior ITF match in November 2008 where she qualified and won her first round match. She had her first ITF win at the US$10k event in Sunderland, UK aged 14 years and nine months. Laura also played for the first time in the Wimbledon main draw in 2009, where she was defeated in three sets by Slovakian top 20 player Daniela Hantuchova 3-6, 6-4, 6-2.

Robson is one of the most prodigious talents to emerge in British tennis for many years, and if she continues to play at the level she has demonstrated, she is on track to emerge as a top player on the main Tour.

Britain's Laura Robson in action at Wimbledon

Robson at the 2009 US Open Junior Girl's Championship, where she progressed to the semi-finals

Gael Monfils, now a top ranked player on the men's tour

DID YOU KNOW?
In 2009, when Kristina Mladenovic won the junior girl's singles title at Roland Garros she became the fourteenth French player to win the title.

DID YOU KNOW?
Frenchman Gael Monfils won the boys singles title at three of the four Junior Grand Slam events in 2004.

Roger Federer won junior Wimbledon in 1998 and Andy Roddick won 2000 Australian Open boys singles title.

As well as the annual junior calendar and the Grand Slams, there are two other prestigious junior events. Both take place at the end of the year in the USA.

The Orange Bowl is an ITF Junior Championship that was first played in 1962 with two divisions, under-12 and under-14, for both boys and girls. Chris Evert, Jimmy Connors, Monica Seles, Andre Agassi and Steffi Graf all played at the event. In 2007 British junior George Morgan won the under-14s boys event.

The Eddie Herr International Junior Tennis Championships is the largest international junior tennis tournament in the world. Founded in 1987, the competition featured four age categories: 18 and under, 16 and under, 14 and under and 12 and under. Andy Roddick won the 18 boys and under event in 1999, while Maria Shrapaova won the 16 and under girls event in 2000. British starlet Laura Robson won the 14 and under event in 2007 after winning the 12 and under event in 2006. Another British girl, Tara Moore, won the 12 and under event in 2004.

Making the transition from playing junior events to the senior circuit places a lot of demands on a player. But there are plenty of today's top players whose name first appeared on the roll of honour as a junior. ●

One of Poland's young players, Agnieska Radwanska

TO FIND OUT MORE ABOUT COMPETING IN BRITISH COMPETITIONS log on to www.lta.org.uk/competition

GET INVOLVED

It is really easy to start playing tennis, either for fun or to enter competitions

There are many places where you can go and play tennis: parks, clubs, schools, leisure centres. All you need to do is find a court. If you find a tennis coach you might consider having a few lessons to get you going. A good coach can explain all the main grips and strokes and get you hitting lots of balls.

One of the most frustrating parts of learning to play is the fact that unless you hit with someone who can already play, you might spend a lot of time picking up balls. To help, try playing with slower bouncing balls. In the UK, juniors play mini tennis, which takes a player through a progression of court sizes and different coloured balls. Don't be afraid as a young adult or a complete beginner to play with a slower bouncing ball. In the long run you will probably learn faster because in no time you will be hitting more balls than you have to pick up.

Once you have mastered the main strokes you might want to consider entering competitions. You may find a competition ladder at a tennis club or park. Once you have signed up, you play a series of matches and then progress up and down the ladder dependent on how many matches you win.

The Lawn Tennis Association (LTA) is the home of British tennis and organises a series of competitions for all levels of play. The best way to get involved with these is to become a British tennis member. You will then be assigned a rating, which means that you would only play matches against players of a similar standard. The rating system extends at the lowest end from 10.2 to 1.1. The good thing about this system is that it allows you to progress up the ratings as you get better and you are guaranteed to play similar level players. Tennis can be a frustrating game if you don't know how good (or bad!) your opponent is.

> ❝ **It's the discipline and the relentlessness of it all that I remember. I felt like I was a professional from about the age of eight** ❞
>
> TIM HENMAN, FORMER WORLD NO.4 AND BRITISH NO.1

BRITISH TENNIS RATINGS

There are 20 ratings bands that cover all levels of player. 10.2 is the lowest and 1.1 is the highest.

BRITISH COMPETITION GRADES

There are 7 grades in the UK. Grade 7 is the lowest and Grade 1 is the highest.

Tim Henman, the former British No.1 and world-ranked player

Andy Murray, on the beach in Melbourne, Australia, 2009

Starting young is vital if you are going to be a professional

Once you have a British tennis rating you can also obtain a ranking that compares you with other players. So in the same way the players on the pro Tour are ranked, so are you. Andy Murray has a world ranking as well as a British ranking. He is the British No.1 player.

If you want to find out more, visit the British Tennis website at www.lta.org.uk. When you start to play tennis you must make sure you hit lots of balls, have fun and, if you want to compete, ensure you play a similar standard player.

If you think you have potential to play tennis at a really high level it is likely that you will progress through certain stages at certain ages. The International Tennis Federation (ITF) organises junior level tennis. Once you have played British tennis events at local, regional and national level a player can start playing ITF tournaments. For juniors (under 18 years of age) these are graded one to five (five being the weakest). These tournaments prepare a player for life on the ITF circuit – the first rung on the professional ladder.

As an adult (over 18) you can also play local, regional and national tournaments and then ITF tournaments. The ITF also organises events for seniors (classified as over 35 years of age) and players with disabilities.

If you are going to play tennis at a professional level it is most likely that you will start playing at a young age. As Tim Henman former world No.4 and British No. 1 says: "It's the discipline and the relentlessness of it all that I remember. I felt like I was a professional from about the age of eight. My school holidays were always about tournaments and where I was going to play."

The career path may vary slightly as everyone develops at different rates, but all the top professionals start playing and are dedicated from an early age. Even if you are not interested in playing professional tennis, tennis is a sport that can be enjoyed at many levels and it is easy to get involved. ●

Britain's Paralympian Lucy Shuker started playing wheelchair tennis in 2003

TO FIND SOMEWHERE TO PLAY TENNIS
log on to
www2.lta.org.uk/Search/FindAClub/
or www.eparktennis.com

Lots of practice is essential

ESSENTIAL KIT

Get the basics: the right racket and tennis shoes

ROGER FEDERER

SERIOUS ABOUT KIT?
Get advice from a tennis coach or a specialist racket retailer.

RACKET WEIGHT GUIDE

Beginners	up to 270g
Intermediates	270 - 300g
Advanced	305g and up

RACKET JARGON

GRIP SIZE – the size of the grip on the handle

HEAD HEAVY – the balance point of the racket is closest to the head

HEAD LIGHT – the balance point is closer to the handle

HEAD SIZE – the size of the string surface

SWEET SPOT – the centre of the racket strings

RACKET

The racket is the most important piece of tennis equipment, and there are a few important factors to consider when trying to find your perfect model.

The first is racket weight. Although modern rackets are generally much lighter than their wooden and graphite ancestors, most manufacturers produce a range of models of varying weights. Some professional players use rackets that weigh over 305 grams – and some even add weight to the frame – but beginners are advised to start with a lighter racket, probably up to 270 grams, to aid the swing and avoid injury.

Second is the size of the handle, or grip size. Most rackets are available in a variety of grip sizes, with the circumference of the handle used to standardise the measurement. Manufacturers cater for sizes below 4 inches for juniors up to 4 $^7/_8$ inches for large adults. It is important to get the right racket size to prevent wrist and elbow strains.

The weight distribution within the frame – the balance – can have a major impact on what it feels like to play with a racket. Head-heavy rackets help a player generate power during drives and serves, but are less stable for touch shots and volleys.

JUAN MARTIN DEL POTRO

MARIA KIRILENKO

Head-light rackets are easier to control but offer less power.

The size of the racket head – the string surface area – can be anything from 85 square inches on a mid-size racket to 135 square inches on a super oversize racket. The bigger the racket head, the easier it is to make contact with the ball and the easier to hit a shot out of the centre, or sweet spot. Professional players generally use rackets with smaller head sizes, which offer greater control. Oversize heads are ideal for beginners.

When choosing a racket it may be tempting to want the same models as the professionals. Until your game is as good, you are more likely to benefit from something more suited to your level of play, particularly when it comes to head size and racket weight. Many coaches and most specialist racket retailers will allow you to loan 'demo' rackets in order to find your perfect match before you buy.

TENNIS SHOES

If you are planning to play tennis regularly, then it is worth investing in a pair of tennis shoes. They are designed to

DID YOU KNOW?
Yellow tennis balls replaced white balls in 1972, but the All England Club did not introduce yellow balls at Wimbledon until 1986.

support the foot during the types of movement specific to tennis, particularly lateral movements. An 'all-court' tennis shoe typically has a smooth herringboned sole to protect the court surface and a toughened exterior around the toes to prevent players from wearing away the front of the shoe when serving.

Although an all-court shoe can be used on most playing surfaces, specialist shoes are available for different surfaces. Grass court shoes have dimples or spikes on the sole for greater grip, while the sole of an indoor carpet shoe is completely smooth to allow a player to slide a little. All-court shoes are typically hard-wearing to withstand hard-court conditions.

CLOTHING

There is plenty of choice on offer when it comes to what you wear on court. You may not need any specialist tennis clothing when starting out, but if you are going to play a lot then good sports kit is worth having. It will keep you cool as you work out and ensure you are comfortable.

BALLS

For any location and court type there is a variety of ball available, but in general a ball from a good manufacturer will play consistently. If you are just starting the game you could consider playing with a slower ball than a standard issue yellow ball. It means while you are perfecting your technique you will enjoy more rallies.

STRINGS

All rackets play better with fresh strings. So even if you don't break a string re-stringing the racket reaps benefits. The general wisdom is to re-string the racket the same number of times during a year as you play in a week – if you play twice a week string your racket twice a year.

GRIPS

Grips are susceptible to wear and tear, and it is worth re-gripping your racket before it becomes too worn, as the handle may become slippery. Many players buy disposable overgrips to preserve their main grip and provide a little more cushioning for their hands.

Andy Roddick has one of the biggest serves in the game

THE SERVE

The serve starts every game and, thanks to technology, is now the most devastating stroke

The serve is by far the most important – and glamorous – stroke in tennis because it's the shot players hit the most once they start competing: statistically, tennis players use their serve more than any other shot.

A big serve is a great asset in today's power game and those with the most effective deliveries find themselves at a huge advantage, particularly on fast surfaces such as grass, indoor carpet and quick hard courts.

The rules of the game allow players two serves per point so if they miss their first delivery they get another chance – a second serve – to get the ball in play. If the ball clips the net on its way over and still lands in the service box the point is stopped and the server gets another serve.

Since servers get two chances to get the ball into their opponent's service box,

generally speaking, first serves are normally hit harder and more aggressively than second serves. Players often try to hit the ball as hard as they can with their first serve but go for more consistency with their second delivery.

Developments in racket and string technology over the years have allowed players to hit the ball harder and harder. These developments in equipment have also meant players can hit the ball with more spin – topspin or slice – for greater control.

While a powerful serve is important, particularly in men's tennis, players that can serve intelligently can also be very effective. Roger Federer is a good example of this – the Swiss star is missing from the top of the big serving leaderboard but because he varies his serve and is one of the most accurate on the men's Tour he is still able to dominate

opponents and hold serve with ease.

There are three basic serves used in the game – a flat serve, a slice serve and a topspin, or kick, serve. The names describe the type of spin players put on the ball – a flat serve has little or no spin and its bounce will be relatively true when it comes off the court. Flat serves also tend to be the most powerful type of serve. A topspin serve is hit by brushing the strings up the back of the ball to make it bounce, or 'kick', up and away from the returner when it comes off the court.

SERVING JARGON

ACE – a winning serve that the returner doesn't touch

DOUBLE FAULT – when the server misses both serves

BREAK POINT – when the returner stands at game point

LET – when the ball clips the net but still lands inside the service box

HOLDING SERVE – when the server wins the game

BREAKING SERVE – when the returner wins the game

KICK – a serve hit with lots of topspin

SLIDER – a serve hit with a lot of slice

RECORD BREAKER ★

Venus Williams holds the record for the fastest ever women's serve in the main draw of a professional event. She whacked one down at 129mph (207 kph) against Hungary's Kira Nagy at the 2007 US Open.

THE SERVE

Venus Williams has the biggest first serve in the history of women's tennis. Technically, it is not as pretty as her sister Serena's, but she has an incredibly fast arm combined with an ability to get off the ground which means she can use her height to full advantage.

1 THE GRIP: Imagine shaking hands with the racket – that's a Chopper grip and that is the most effective grip for a serve.

2 A consistent and accurate ball toss is vital. With a smooth action, try to place the ball in the air rather than throwing it and try to put it just in front of your body and slightly to the right (for right-handers).

3 Try to bring the racket up so the strings meet the ball at the highest possible contact point.

4 It's important to keep your eye on the ball throughout the execution of the stroke. If you drop your head it's easy to drag the ball down and into the net.

5 Start the service action with your feet shoulder width apart to form a solid base from which to push upwards.

6 Use your leg muscles to help you push upwards and explode into the shot, lifting you off the ground. The higher your contact point, the better. It will help create more power and help you clear the net consistently.

WATCH OUT FOR FOOT FAULTS!

If either of your feet touches the baseline before you hit the ball a foot fault will be called and your serve will be illegal. Don't stand too close to the centre mark on the baseline either – if you stray to the 'wrong' side that's also a foot fault.

A slice serve is hit by bringing the racket face around the side of the ball. The result is a serve that 'slides' away from an opponent – particularly effective on fast and low bouncing surfaces such as grass.

To achieve maximum power, serves are hit overarm but it is in fact legal to put the ball into play underarm as multi-Grand Slam champion Martina Hingis once famously did against Steffi Graf in the 1999 French Open final.

The game has featured many big servers over the years. John McEnroe was one of the most effective, not necessarily because of the power the American generated, but because of his placement and vicious outswinging left-handed slice serves. Germany's Boris Becker was one of the first really big servers and was quickly nicknamed 'Boom Boom' by the press as he bombarded his way to the 1985 Wimbledon title aged just 17. Then there was 14-time Grand Slam winner Pete Sampras, who had one of the biggest ever serves. More recently, another American, Andy Roddick, has been the biggest server around and then there's 6' 10" (208cm) Ivo Karlovic, one of the most difficult to face simply because of the angles the Croatian can create from such a tall frame. In the women's game Martina Navratilova's tricky left-handed delivery helped her claim 59 Grand Slam titles and over the last few years the Williams sisters – Venus and Serena – have blasted their way to success by possessing two of the biggest serves ever seen. ●

Serena Williams follows through after striking a powerful forehand

THE GAME'S GREAT FOREHANDS

Rafael Nadal
Roger Federer →
Ivan Lendl
Fernando Verdasco
Robin Soderling
Fernando Gonzalez
Serena Williams
Juan Carlos Ferrero
Steffi Graf
Juan Martin del Potro →
Ana Ivanovic

THE FOREHAND

Players use this shot to go on the attack. It can be an effective weapon especially when hit with big topspin.

Multi-Grand Slam winning Spaniard Rafael Nadal has many attributes, numerous elements to his game that make him one of the best ever to pick up a racket. But if you were to ask his peers to choose the one strength that makes him so dangerous most would say his forehand.

Nadal hits the ball incredibly hard, but it is the way he hits the ball that sets him apart. The man from Mallorca has ferocious racket head speed that creates huge topspin, which in turn makes the ball fly off the surface of the court and take opponents way behind the baseline

and out of position. They say that once Rafa gets his opponent on the run with his cross-court and 'inside-out' forehands there is only ever one winner of the point.

However, forehands such as Nadal's are a relatively new addition to the game. Players learning the sport as recently as 20 years ago wouldn't have been taught to play the stroke the way Nadal does. 'Closed stance' forehands were the only forehands hit and taught. Players would hit the ball with their upper body and legs sideways on to the court and step into the shot and towards their target area as they struck the ball. Most coaches will argue every player

should still be able to hit a closed stance forehand and that it's the right way to hit the ball in certain circumstances (on short balls for example), but most of the time players now hit forehands with an 'open stance'. An open stance forehand differs in that the shoulders and torso rotate as the player hits the ball so they make contact with their upper and lower body facing the net.

Another difference between forehands past and present is the spin put on the ball and swing shape. Traditionally, players were taught to swing the racket from low to high and finish with the racket pointing towards their target area. Now players such as Nadal whip the

THE FOREHAND

Chile's Fernando Gonzalez has one of the biggest forehands in the game. Once the South American goes on the attack, there are few who can live with his power.

A full western forehand grip

FERNANDO GONZALEZ

1 THE GRIP: There are several ways of holding the racket to play a forehand. Gonzales has what is known as a full western grip which allows him to put a lot of spin on the ball.

2 Fernando makes contact with the ball in the perfect hitting zone — out in front of his body to create power, and not too close or too far away from his body so he's balanced when he strikes the ball.

3 This picture is taken a fraction of a second before contact. Notice that the racket head is coming from below the height of the ball. The strings will brush up the back of the ball at high speed to create vicious topspin that will control the flight of the ball.

4 Throughout the shot Gonzalez uses his non-racket hand (left hand) to help with his balance.

5 Use lots of quick steps to get into the correct hitting position for every shot.

6 Gonzo has great rotation as he hits the ball. He begins the stroke by coiling his upper body like a spring and unloads his entire body into the ball for greater power.

7 The South American will have begun the stroke with his knees slightly bent. Now his legs are fully extended — he is exploding upwards and into the shot as his body rotates.

8 His head is still throughout the stroke and his eyes are fixed on the ball. Always watch the ball!

racket across their bodies with what is know as a 'windscreen wiper' follow through which ends on the opposite side of their body with the racket head back down around waist height.

Pros hit the ball with much more spin nowadays too, largely because of the different way they hold the racket and advances in racket and string technology. Rafael Nadal has a forehand grip known as "full western". If you picked up the racket as if you were shaking hands with it and then twisted the racket another ninety degrees in your hand you will have the same grip. It allows the player to put a huge amount of topspin on the ball.

One type of forehand that every player should try to learn is the "inside out" forehand, which is struck from the backhand side of the court. This requires some nimble footwork to get 'around' the ball and into position, but allows players to dominate the rally without having to use their normally weaker backhand. It does not replace a backhand. ●

GOLDEN RULES

1. **Prepare early and get your racket back quickly.**
2. **Keep your eyes on the ball.**
3. **Transfer your weight into the shot for optimum power.**

Rafael Nadal has a dangerous forehand

Richard Gasquet prepares to unleash his single-handed backhand. You can see here how far he turns his shoulder to get enough power

THE GAME'S GREAT BACKHANDS

Justine Henin →
Richard Gasquet
Carla Suarez Navarro
Stefan Edberg
Elena Dementieva
Chris Evert
Roger Federer
Andy Murray →
Gustavo Kuerten

THE BACKHAND

This can be a difficult shot to master but in theory it is easier than a forehand. Whether one hand or two, plenty of players count it as their best shot

For most people that pick up a tennis racket, the backhand is the hardest shot to master, but for those lucky enough to be blessed with good technique it can be their strongest weapon.

In theory it should be easy to execute for it involves a much more natural motion than the forehand. Think about it for a moment — the way the arm moves away from the upper body when hitting a backhand is the same action as used when putting dinner plates down on a table or releasing a car seat belt.

The problem, however, is that for most players the backhand motion is simply physically weaker than the action they use to strike a forehand and so the stroke is more inconsistent and less effective when they try to go on the attack. Many players try to solve this problem by hitting the ball with two hands on the racket when playing a backhand. By adding an extra hand they can create more power, find it easier to take the ball on the rise (particularly on the return of serve) and gain greater control over the direction of the ball.

There are several advantages to hitting with one hand. One-handed

THE RETURN OF SERVE

Groundstrokes are used once a rally is under way, but also at the start of a point with a return of serve when the returner tries to get the serve back. The same technique as a normal groundstroke can be used, but the returner should keep their take-back short and try not to take as big a swing at the ball. Just concentrate on getting the ball back into play!

THE BACKHAND

The 2008 Olympic champion Elena Dementieva is one of the cleanest ball strikers in the game from the back of the court. Like many of the women players, the Russian favours two hands and uses her backhand to soak up pressure and also go on the attack when the opportunity comes along.

ELENA DEMENTIEVA

1 Elena will have turned her shoulders and upper body to prepare for her backhand and when she's ready to hit the ball she will rotate through the shot to add power to the strike.

2 Like all great players, Elena keeps her head still and watches the ball from start to finish.

3 To achieve maximum power and control try to make contact out of the middle of the strings – the sweetspot of the racket.

4 To create topspin, bring the racket head from underneath the ball and brush up the back of the ball with the strings. Good racket head speed is important to create maximum spin. Her swing will have started low and finish high on the opposite side of her body.

5 Her trunk is side on but rotating fast so it will open up as she follows through.

6 Her weight is transferring forward and up through her right leg as she makes contact.

7 Good footwork is extremely important when hitting backhands. Try to get into the right position by using lots of small, quick steps around the ball. For players with double handed backhands this is very important as they cannot stretch out to reach a ball as easily as a player with a single handed backhand.

8 She makes contact in a comfortable position – not too close or too far away from her body and between knee and chest high.

9 To get the racket face in the correct position on contact it's important to hold the racket with the right grip.

players have the luxury of a bit more reach when stretched wide and they find it easier to put slice on the ball (a shot normally played with just one hand) when they play on low-bouncing or fast court surfaces. Players who hit with two hands can find it difficult to take one hand off the racket to hit a one-handed slice, which is an essential shot to add variety and consistency to a player's baseline game.

So who has a nice backhand in today's game? There's not much wrong with any aspect of Roger Federer's tennis – he has a majestic one-handed topspin backhand drive and can hit a mean slice too. Frenchman Richard Gasquet's one-hander is another fine example, and in the women's game Amelie Mauresmo and Spanish clay-courter Carla Suarez Navarro hit the ball very cleanly using one hand. Belgian former world No.1 Justine Henin's single-handed backhand was admired the world over.

Of the two-handers around, Federer's great rival Rafael Nadal has a fabulous cross-court backhand. Despite him playing tennis with his left hand, he is actually right-handed which is a key element of his double-hander, as he is able to use the strength and control of his right arm to aggressively pull the ball back across court when out of position.

Andy Murray has a great two-handed backhand as he is able to change direction with devastating effect. Opponents find it very difficult to tell whether he is about to hit cross court or down the line and the ability to add disguise on the backhand is another important factor in dominating from the back of the court. ●

Top Croatian player Marin Cilic watches the ball as he prepares to play the volley

GOLDEN RULES

1. Turn your shoulders, meet the ball out in front.
2. Create a wide base by stepping into the shot.
3. Make sure your upper body doesn't collapse forward after contact.

THE VOLLEY

There's nothing more satisfying than finishing a point with an aggressive, killer volley at the net!

THE GAME'S GREAT VOLLEYERS

Boris Becker
Stefan Edberg
Pete Sampras
Pat Rafter
Pat Cash
Tim Henman →
Martina Navratilova
Jana Novotna
Hana Mandlikova
Amelie Mauresmo
Martina Hingis →
Andy Murray
Lisa Raymond

Tennis fans watching professionals play the game 10 or 20 years ago would have seen many more points finished at the net with volleys – when a player takes the ball out of the air before it bounces on their side of the court – or overheads than we do now. Back then, the tennis balls that were used on the professional Tours were slightly smaller, a bit faster through the air and some say even the grass at Wimbledon played faster than it does today, which all played into the hands of those players brave enough to venture into the net. They could break down opponents by hitting an aggressive approach shot off a short ball and follow it into the net to cut off their opponent's reply with a winning volley.

As racket and string technology moved on, though, it became easier for the "baseliners" (players who stay mainly at the back of the court) to hit powerful forehand and backhand passing shots struck with masses of spin. These developments signalled the end of serve and volley tennis and today the sport is dominated by players with big serves and big groundstrokes (forehands and backhands) – rarely do you see the pros venturing into the net unless they have no choice and have been lured in by a dropshot.

Some of the best ever to play the game became world-beaters thanks to their effective volleying. On the women's side, Martina Navratilova changed the way

THE VOLLEY

AMELIE MAURESMO

Mauresmo is one of the few female pros who regularly comes forward to finish points from the net. The two-time Grand Slam-winning Frenchwoman has a classic style of play which is admired by tennis fans all over the world.

1 The correct grip for a volley is the same as for a serve (see page 105) . You can use this grip on the backhand and forehand volley. This is essential because there's no time to change grips at the net. You can also use the same grip for the smash too.

2 Positioning at the net is important. This picture shows Amelie hitting a first volley so she's still quite far back when she makes contact – around the service line. Generally speaking, you should be around two or three metres from the net – too close and you'll be lobbed, too far away and you'll find yourself playing every volley off your toes!

3 The racket face should be slightly open on contact to create slice. Putting spin on the ball will help control your shot and keep it low when it comes off the court. Try to cut down the back of the ball.

4 As with any shot in tennis, try to keep your head still during the stroke (this will help with balance) and watch the ball like a hawk from start to finish.

5 Keep the racket head above the wrist on contact with the ball.

6 She has created a fantastic wide base by stepping into the shot. This helps her balance as she hits the ball.

7 She has transferred her weight into the shot by stepping onto her right foot as she makes contact. Afterwards she will keep moving forwards to cut down the angles for her opponent.

8 Try to build a shoulder turn into your technique – it will help your accuracy and stop you pulling the ball across your body.

9 Notice how Amelie uses her non-racket hand to help her balance. She is in complete control of her body when she makes contact with the ball. Her arms work together in perfect symmetry.

10 Try to make contact with the ball in the perfect hitting position – out in front of your body and a comfortable distance away from it. If the ball is too close or far away you'll find yourself off-balance.

tennis was played by bringing her physicality to the court, and her power allowed her to dominate opponents with her big serve and attacking net play. It was her love of coming forward on grass (a surface well-suited to attacking tennis because the ball stays nice and low) that helped her collect nine Wimbledon singles titles.

John McEnroe possessed an unusual technique on the volley but it was incredibly effective as he picked opponents apart with his serve-and -volley game. Pete Sampras was another who could back up a big serve with great volleys, but perhaps the two players with the best technique at the net were Sweden's Stefan Edberg, twice a Wimbledon champion in 1988 and 1990, and Britain's Tim Henman, who even reached the semi-finals of

the French Open on clay by unsettling opponents with his 'slice and dice' style of play. In today's game Roger Federer has the ability to hit great volleys, Andy Murray's net play is vastly underestimated (he is perhaps the best volleyer at the top of the men's game) and one of the most comfortable young players at the net is Croatia's Marin Cilic.

All these players have fantastic hand-eye co-ordination, which is essential up at the net where a player's reaction time is vastly reduced and they are all great athletes, blessed with powerful legs to help them get down low to dipping balls. They also posess wonderful balance and what tennis players call 'soft' hands, the ability to control volleys by placing them in exactly the right spots. ●

DID YOU KNOW?

For the first time in 2009 the women's Tour allowed players to call for their coach to come on court between sets at all tournaments, except the Grand Slams.

Nick Bollettieri makes a point to Serena Williams

HOW TO FIND A CLUB LEVEL COACH

Log onto www.lta.org.uk and search for a coach in your area.

COACHING

There are many high-profile coaches on the Tour who assist players with developing their game technically, tactically and sometimes mentally

The relationship between a professional tennis player and his coach is a unique one. While in team sports like football, basketball or baseball the coach is employed by an organisation that functions pretty much like a company, tennis coaches are hired directly by the players. So the situation arises where the coach, who is the boss and should have a commanding position, is in fact the employee in the relationship. The coach gets his pay cheque from the player, not a company. It is a curious relationship and a highly individual one.

Just as every player is an individual, so is their relationship with their coach. Some player-coach relationships last an entire career. The American player James Blake has worked with Brian Barker since he was 12 years old.

Some players change coaches as their needs change. In 2008, Andy Roddick, the former US Open champion, chose to team up with a new coach Larry Stefanki and together they worked on bringing new skills and a new fitness level to Roddick's game.

Some players surround themselves with a team, like Andy Murray. He has a permanent coach, an occasional coach in Alex Corretja, the former Spanish player, as well as a physical conditioner and a physiotherapist. The team spends time together off court as well. Murray has used the team tactically to assist in the development of his game.

The mighty Roger Federer has had no formal coach for most of his career, while

← TOP COACH PROFILE

Nick Bollettieri is one of the world's best tennis coaches. Born in New York, he runs an academy in Florida where he has trained players such as Maria Sharapova and Andre Agassi. He is considered to be one of the most successful and influential coaches in tennis.

DID YOU KNOW?
Judy Murray, mum of Andy and Jamie Murray, is a tennis coach.

JUDY MURRAY

Rafael Nadal with his coach, Uncle Toni, during a practice session

Rafael Nadal has his Uncle Toni as his coach. So there are many different approaches at a professional level.

It is likely that a professional tennis player will have his or her own coach to help develop both tennis technique and tactics and sometimes even become their mentor or greatest supporter. While a coach is often present as a player competes, most development work takes place outside of the tournaments.

A coach and a professional player spend an enormous amount of time together on Tour. They often travel together, spend a lot of hours on court together and sometimes even share the same hotel.

Many players attend academies as juniors and as they are rising up the rankings. Here they benefit from the coaching on offer at an academy such as Nick Bollettieri's Academy in Florida.

There are plenty of other academies around the world that have developed world-class players.

Academies are often set up by former players, like Academia Sanchez-Casal, Spain (where Andy Murray, Svetlana Kuznetsova and Ana Ivanovic were put through their paces), Juan Carlos Ferrero Equelite Tennis Academy, Spain, and The Mouratoglou Tennis Academy, France (which produced Marcos Baghdatis and Nicolas Kiefer).

Club-level players can benefit from coaching sessions. Most facilities that offer tennis will have a coach who can teach all standards of player and probably also group coaching sessions, where you can learn with other players of a similar standard.

Although the professional players on Tour forge relationships with coaches to develop their game, whatever the level of play, tennis is a game where you can keep learning and improving your game. ●

HOW TO BECOME A COACH

There are several routes to becoming a coach. In the UK the Lawn Tennis Association (LTA) has developed a structured career pathway. After initial entry as a coaching assistant, coaches elect to progress as either club coaches or performance coaches. The LTA alongside other organisations provides comprehensive training programmes for coaches. To find out more go to the LTA website to see what is available: www/lta.org.uk/coaches.

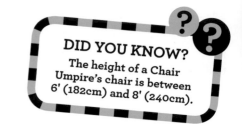

OFFICIATING

The role of Chair Umpires, Line Umpires and Referees is to ensure the passage of fair play for the players

Professional officials employed by the International Tennis Federation (ITF) adjudicate top-level tennis matches. All officials undergo training before they can officiate matches and there is an established career pathway in place at both national and international level.

There are two types of umpire, the Chair Umpire and the Line Umpire. The Chair Umpire is the more senior of the officials. They sit up high in the centre of the court and have overall responsibility for the match. That authority extends, according to the Rules of Tennis to being "the final authority on all questions of fact during the match". Among these duties, which are laid out clearly by the ITF, the Chair Umpire completes the scorecard, the official record of the match and announces the score. The umpire ensures the match is played at a pace that is within the rules.

The Chair Umpire has responsibility for suspending matches due to rain or due to an injury to one of the players and he can call for a doctor if requested by a player. The Chair Umpire can overrule the decisions of the Line Umpires.

Line Umpires sit on court and are responsible for watching a specific line to determine if the ball lands in or out of

The Chair Umpire and player discuss a point during a match

Line umpires file on to take up their positions on court at Wimbledon

ITF CAREER PATHWAY FOR OFFICIALS

LEVEL 1: Basic introduction to officiating, the Rules of the Game and basic techniques of chair and line umpiring. It is administered through national associations. In the UK this is conducted by the LTA.

LEVEL 2: For officials who have some experience and commitment to officiating. Officials that pass a written examination and practical exercises become ITF white badge officials.

LEVEL 3: For officials eligible to operate at international events. Officials become bronze, silver and gold badge holders. Only 25 international officials hold the gold badge.

play. This may be the service box, the sidelines or the baseline. The Line Umpire communicates his decision to the Chair Umpire with a show of hands or with a verbal call.

In matches there is normally a team of Line Umpires who work 75 minutes on and 75 minutes off, to allow them to retain concentration, which can be very important in a long match.

In addition to the umpires all professionally organised tournaments have a referee who works behind the scenes liaising with players and organising such things as the draw and the order of play.

To assist with the assessment of whether a ball in play is "in" or "out" in 2006 the ITF introduced a device called Hawk-Eye to the professional tour. The US Open was the first Grand Slam where this electronic ball monitoring system was used. It provides an instant replay in the event that a player disputes the call of a Line or Chair Umpire. Not all of the players on the Tour like the system, but it is used on most major show courts. It can add an extra dimension to the spectator experience if it is used at a key point. If there is a slight delay with the replay, the spectators wait with baited breath to see the outcome.

There are different rules in tennis dependent on the level of the game, but the ITF sets all of these out very clearly. Many people enjoy officiating matches at the highest level on the Tour or on a national level and even at club level. Officiating tennis matches is one way to have a career in tennis aside from becoming a professional player. ●

Andy Murray stands in front of the big screen during an action replay

HAWKEYE
A player is allowed three incorrect challenges each set and is awarded a further challenge if the set goes to a tie-break.

PLAYERS THAT HAVE TESTED THE UMPIRE

JOHN MCENROE

Famous for on-court tantrums. The greatest of which was probably, "You cannot be serious man. That ball was on the line – chalk flew up!" at Wimbledon in 1981.

MARAT SAFIN

One of the great characters on court, but pity his poor rackets. He smashed many a racket during a match – one season he destroyed more than 100.

GORAN IVANISEVIC

Some put it down to his passion for the sport, but not everyone was fond of his swearing (normally in his native language) and racket smashing.

UK TENNIS EVENTS

There's plenty of live tennis action to watch in the UK. Most of it happens during the summer as Britain is at the centre of the grass-court season

The Championships at Wimbledon are held during the last week of June and the first week of July. There are a series of smaller grass-court events leading up to the major event. For the women there is the AEGON Classic at Edgbaston and for the men the AEGON Championships at Queen's Club. There is a combined event at Eastbourne for both men and women. There are also some great exhibition matches which give spectators an opportunity to see some of the top players in action in a more relaxed environment, most notably at the Boodles Challenge at Stoke Park just outside London, the Fortis Bank Tennis Classic at the Hurlingham Club in London and the Liverpool International.

Depending on the draw, Davis Cup ties are played at venues in the UK. Recent ties have been held in Liverpool, Glasgow, Wimbledon and Eastbourne. Keep an eye on the LTA website to find out about home ties.

From 2009 until 2012 the O2 Arena in London plays host to the Barclays ATP World Tour Finals. This is the end of year event contested by the top eight male singles players and top eight doubles teams in the world. At stake is US$5 million in total prize money, the chance to win one of the most prestigious titles in tennis and to finish as the season's No. 1 player. It is a fantastic event for spectators. The round-robin format followed by knockout semi-finals and final means whatever day you go you are guaranteed to see the world's best players in action. Prior to its arrival in London it was hosted at the Qi Zhong Stadium in Shanghai and after 2012 it may move to a new destination.

In 2012 the Olympic tennis event will be held at the All England Club as part of London 2012. Most other sports events will be hosted mainly at the Olympic site in Stratford, East London.

> **The event has a great history and means so much to the top players. It's great to think the race to the No.1 spot and the title of ATP World Tour Champion could come down to the wire in London**

ANDY MURRAY ON THE BARCLAYS ATP WORLD TOUR FINALS

Andy Murray poses with the trophy after his 7-5, 6-4 victory over American James Blake at Queen's Club in the 2009 AEGON Championships

DID YOU KNOW?
The 2012 Olympic tennis event will be hosted at the All England Club, Wimbledon.

DID YOU KNOW?
In 2009 Andy Murray was the first Briton to win the Queens Club event for 71 years.

Devonshire Park in Eastbourne is the home of the the AEGON International

TOUR EVENTS

THE CHAMPIONSHIPS
Grand Slam Event

DRAW SIZE (MEN):
128 singles, 64 doubles pairs
DRAW SIZE (WOMEN):
128 singles, 64 doubles pairs

AEGON CHAMPIONSHIPS
ATP World Tour 250 Event
The Queen's Club London – June

DRAW SIZE: 56 singles, 24 doubles pairs
WEBSITE: www.aegonchampionships.com

AEGON CLASSIC
WTA International Event
Edgbaston Priory Club, Birmingham – June

DRAW SIZE: 56 singles, 24 doubles pairs
WEBSITE: www.lta.org.uk

AEGON INTERNATIONAL
ATP World Tour 250/WTA Premier Event
Devonshire Park, Eastbourne – June

DRAW SIZE (MEN):
32 singles, 16 doubles pairs
DRAW SIZE (WOMEN):
32 singles, 16 doubles pairs
WEBSITE: www.lta.org.uk

BARCLAYS ATP WORLD TOUR FINALS
O2 Arena, Docklands, London – November

DRAW SIZE (MEN): Top 8 men's singles and top 8 doubles pairs
WEBSITE:
www.barclaysatpworldtourfinals.com

EXHIBITION EVENTS

THE BOODLES CHALLENGE
Men's Exhibition Event
Stoke Park Club, Buckinghamshire – June

WEBSITE: www.theboodles.com

THE FORTIS BANK TENNIS CLASSIC
Men's/Seniors Exhibition Event
Hurlingham Club, London – June

WEBSITE: www.fortistennisclassic.com

THE TRADITION I-CAP
Liverpool International Men's/Women's Seniors Exhibition Event
Calderstones Park Liverpool – June

WEBSITE: www.liverpooltennis.co.uk

AEGON MASTERS TENNIS
ATP Tour of Champions finale (Seniors)
Royal Albert Hall, London – December

WEBSITE: www.aegon masterstennis.com

No two days are the same for a professional tennis player but if they are in action at a tournament there are certain routines that a player will follow

A DAY IN THE LIFE OF ANNE KEOTHAVONG

PLAYER PROFILE

Full Name	Anne Keothavong
Date of Birth	September 16 1983
Place of Birth	London, England
Height	5' 9" (175cm)
Weight	137lbs (62kg)
Plays	Right-handed, two-handed backhand
Turned Pro	2001
Website	www.annekeothavong.co.uk

H ere's how a competition day unfolds for top British player and world-ranked Anne Keothavong.

8am

Anne wakes up and has a match scheduled to be the last of the day, so she's not sure what time she will play, but knows it will be much later. She eats breakfast with her coach, which on match day consists of poached eggs on toast and some fruit and plenty to drink, one coffee in the morning and juice and water.

DID YOU KNOW?

In 2009 Anne Keothavong became the first woman for 16 years to break into the top 50 of the singles world rankings with a career high listing of 48.

9.45am

After a short time spent relaxing and getting her kit together for a hit Anne heads off to the practice courts. As her match is scheduled late she will hit twice before she plays her match, once in the morning for 45 minutes and then again just before the match to get loosened up. En route to the courts she will pick up her rackets, which have been re-strung overnight in preparation for the match.

11.30am

Anne's on-court practice is preceded by a 10-minute jog in the gym, some exercises for the shoulder and some short, sharp sprints. In total this would be about 20 minutes of exercise.

Anne then practises on court for 45 minutes. At a tournament where the courts are busy, she and her hitting partner may have to share a court with another competitor. If she will be playing a left-hander she will try and hit with another leftie to get her eye in. She will practise some serves, hit some groundstrokes and practise some volleys.

> **66 Wimbledon is my favourite tournament. It's on home turf and that's where you get the most support 99**

DID YOU KNOW?

Anne grew up playing tennis in her local park in North London.

12.30pm

After her first practice session if her body has any little niggles she may have a session with the physiotherapist. She will take a shower and eat some lunch. Lunch on a match day would consist of salad, pasta or rice, vegetables and maybe some chicken.

1pm

Although she does not know what precise time her match will start, Anne likes to relax, either at the players' hotel if it is near to the tournament or if that's too far away in the players' lounge at the match ground. Anne has to keep an eye on the score of the matches underway on her court.

4pm

Once it is nearly time to play Anne will have another hit for 20-30 minutes to get her body moving again. If she is with another British player she may hit with them, someone like Sarah Borwell who might also be her doubles partner. Then after the hit and just before going on court she will have a final talk about tactics with her coach. Anne likes to be alone immediately before the match.

5.30pm

Waiting in the locker room, Anne will have one eye on the score of the match that's underway and have a snack, maybe a powerbar or half a sandwich. Then she will start warming up. Anne likes to listen to music immediately before playing. She gets the call to court from the referee over the tannoy in the player's area and then she will meet her opponent outside the referee's office and head off to the court.

7.30pm

Once the match is complete at a WTA event there is a requirement for a player to attend a press conference within 45 minutes to an hour of finishing the match. A player may choose to go straight to face the press if they want to leave the grounds as soon as possible. There's also a need to cool down and do some stretching.

In the press conference accredited members of the media can ask about all aspects of the match and how the player saw it. There might be some discussion of the key points and then some discussion about the next opponent. This allows the journalists to write a match report that reflects how the player saw the match as well as how it unfolded from the press box.

10pm

Win or lose a match, there is always the next day to consider and so after dinner there's maybe a chat with friends or some time alone. During a tournament it is always important to get plenty of rest so Anne will get to sleep before it all starts again. ●

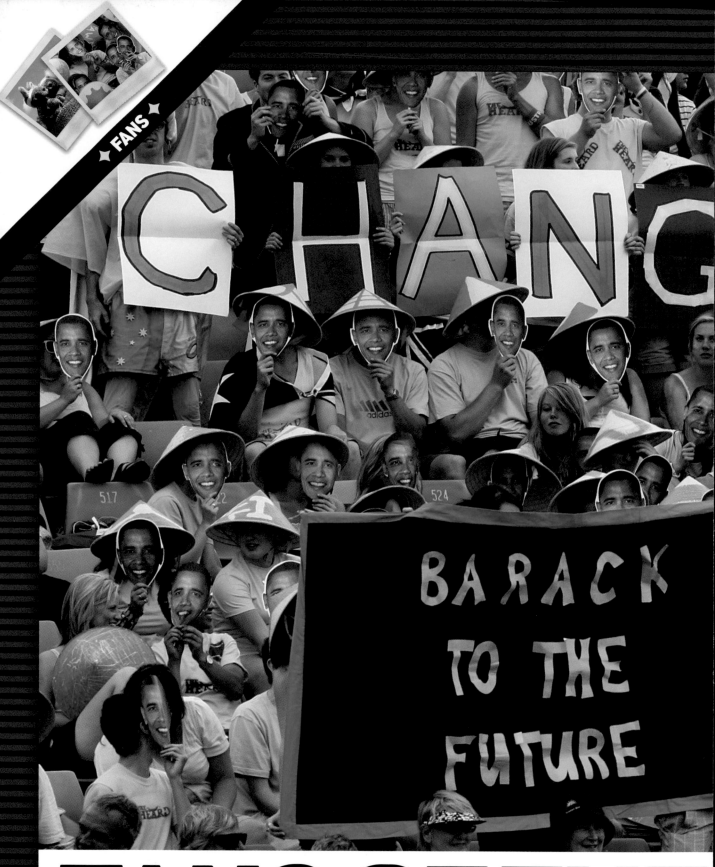

FANS OF THE

In the shade at the Australian Open

Australian fans acknowledge the inauguration of US President Barack Obama during the 2009 Australian Open

WORLD

Wimbledon spectators may be famously quiet during play but around the world, tennis fans can be quite raucous and very colourful. Individual players have their own following wherever they play, who are waiting for a glimpse of their favourite player either on or off court. Come Davis or Fed Cup, when it's one country against another, the atmosphere can be electric as the fans cheer on their national tennis team. ●

FANS

Clowning around

Spanish fans at
the Australian Open

An Australian fan
waits for action

British supporter
at Wimbledon

Wot no Roof ?
Wimbledon 2007

Green and Gold of Australia

Croatian fans cheer
on their man

"Please can
I have your
autograph?"

Britain's Andy Murray parades the 2009 trophy at the AEGON Championships held at Queen's Club, London

ACKNOWLEDGEMENTS

The research for this book has been assisted by the wealth of websites and books that are currently published on tennis. I am indebted to tennis historian and legendary journalist Bud Collins for his *History of Tennis*. If you decide you would like to find out more, there is no better comprehensive tennis history book than Bud's.

There are official and unofficial player biographies, some more enjoyable than others, but one that caught my eye for its wonderful combination of words, images and inspiration was *The World of Rafael Nadal* by Luca Appino, published by Flora Consulting and presented by manufacturer Babolat. Then there's a whole world of information on individual player websites and those of the sports governing bodies; atpworldtour.com; sonyericssonwtatourcom; itf.com and for information about tennis in Great Britain, lta.org.uk. Thanks to the communications teams at the governing bodies for their assistance. Also tennishead. net is a useful website and magazine.

Specific reference sources are:
- *The Bud Collins History of Tennis* (New Chapter Press)
- *Wimbledon Compendium* by Alan Little (The All England Tennis and Croquet Club)
- *ITF Davis Cup Media Guide* (International Tennis Federation)
- *Official Guide to Men's Professional Tennis* (ATP World Tour)
- *Sony Ericsson WTA Tour Official Guide* (WTA Tour)
- *The Book of Tennis* (Chris Bowers, JWM)